JENNIF[ER]

When Dreams Fall Apart

HOW UNANSWERED PRAYERS CAN
DEEPEN YOUR INTIMACY WITH GOD

MOODY PUBLISHERS
CHICAGO

© 2025 by
JENNIFER LUCY TYLER

All rights reserved. No part of this book may be reproduced in any form without permission in writing from the publisher, except in the case of brief quotations embodied in critical articles or reviews.

Scripture quotations have been taken from the Christian Standard Bible®, Copyright © 2017 by Holman Bible Publishers. Used by Permission. Christian Standard Bible® and CSB© are federally registered trademarks of Holman Bible Publishers.

All emphasis to Scripture has been added.

The author is represented by Alive Literary Agency, www.aliveliterary.com.

Edited by Pamela Joy Pugh
Interior design: Koko Toyama
Cover design: Good Mood Design Co / Riley Moody
Cover texture of collage posters © 2025 by NKate / Creative Market. All rights reserved.
Author photo: Bolden Photography

Library of Congress Cataloging-in-Publication Data

Names: Tyler, Jennifer Lucy author
Title: When dreams fall apart : how unanswered prayers can deepen your
  intimacy with God / Jennifer Lucy Tyler.
Description: Chicago : Moody Publishers, [2025] | Includes bibliographical
  references. | Summary: "Readers observe the moments in Scripture when
  people cried out to God, but His answer was delayed or different than
  they'd expected. Together with Tyler, readers learn to name and lament
  their unanswered prayers, and they discover pathways to resilient hope,
  faithful contentment, and triumphant joy"-- Provided by publisher.
Identifiers: LCCN 2025019050 (print) | LCCN 2025019051 (ebook) | ISBN
  9780802435521 paperback | ISBN 9780802469557 ebook
Subjects: LCSH: Trust in God--Christianity--Biblical teaching |
  Hope--Religious aspects--Christianity | Suffering--Religious
  aspects--Christianity | Grief--Religious aspects--Christianity | BISAC:
  RELIGION / Christian Living / Personal Growth | RELIGION / Christian
  Living / Death, Grief, Bereavement
Classification: LCC BV4637 .T954 2025 (print) | LCC BV4637 (ebook) | DDC
  248.4--dc23/eng/20250708
LC record available at https://lccn.loc.gov/2025019050
LC ebook record available at https://lccn.loc.gov/2025019051

Originally delivered by fleets of horse-drawn wagons, the affordable paperbacks from D. L. Moody's publishing house resourced the church and served everyday people. Now, after more than 125 years of publishing and ministry, Moody Publishers' mission remains the same—even if our delivery systems have changed a bit. For more information on other books (and resources) created from a biblical perspective, go to www.moodypublishers.com or write to:

Moody Publishers
820 N. LaSalle Boulevard
Chicago, IL 60610

1 3 5 7 9 10 8 6 4 2

Printed in the United States of America

*I dedicate this book to one of my answered prayers,
Justice Joy Tyler.*

May you never doubt the character of God as you walk through all that comes with living.

The Lord knows you, sees you, and is with you always.

I also dedicate this book to my mother, Robin Schumpert, the woman who taught me what it looks like to trust God when everything seemingly has fallen apart. You continue to guide me through your example today.

*Love you deeply,
JLT*

Contents

Foreword	9
Chapter 1: Barren	11
Chapter 2: Lament	25
Chapter 3: Exile	43
Chapter 4: Traverse	63
Chapter 5: Prodigal	83
Chapter 6: Manifest	99
Chapter 7: Promises	119
Chapter 8: Remember	139
Chapter 9: Rebuild	153
Chapter 10: Glory	169
Epilogue: The Other Side	187
Acknowledgments	191
Notes	193

Foreword

I HAVE THIS THING ABOUT John the Baptist.

I love him. I'm obsessed with him.

In fact, as a term of respect and friendship, I like to call him JTB.

The thing about JTB is this: his ministry wasn't the kind of dream most people long for today. He was sent by God to prepare the way for his cousin: the Savior of the world. He was destined for a set-apart (read: strange) life, and his ministry didn't culminate in comfort or acclaim. He was beheaded by a tyrant and his vengeful wife.

There's a moment near the end of his life when he sends word to Jesus. It's one of the rawest encounters in Scripture, a desperate question from a man whose dream seems to be unraveling.

In the gospel of Matthew, we read that JTB sends his disciples to ask Jesus, *"Are you the one who is to come, or should we expect someone else?"* We don't know exactly what drove the very man who baptized Jesus, who saw the Spirit descend and heard the voice of the Father thunder from heaven to question His identity. But I imagine it had something to do with the death of his own dream: the promise of pain becoming reality as he sat in prison for his faithfulness.

Jesus sends word back to reassure him. And then, after John's disciples leave, Jesus turns to the crowd and says the most intimate, human thing: that there is no one born of a woman greater than John. In essence, He essentially says: guys, John is the best.

As soon as I met my friend Jennifer Lucy Tyler, I started calling her JLT, in honor of JTB.

She carries a wild authority, paired with a grace and compassion unlike any other minister of the gospel I know. She will point you to truth without flinching, and she will comfort you without hesitation. And like John, I believe her voice has been forged through suffering. Her wisdom is hard-won. Her leadership is evidence of God's faithfulness in her life.

JTB knew something about dreams that fall apart.

JLT does too.

If you're holding this book, my guess is that you do as well. I certainly do.

Jennifer Lucy Tyler has been the friend and leader I needed on the hardest days of my life. She has lovingly pointed me back to Jesus and reminded me: He is the one we've been waiting for. He is who He says He is. He is still good.

You're in good hands under her guidance.

I'm so glad you're here.

JESS CONNOLLY
Founder of Go and Tell Gals; author of *Breaking Free from Body Shame* and *Tired of Being Tired*

1

Barren

HAVE YOU EVER PRAYED, AND heaven seems silent? And you begin wondering if God truly hears when you pray?

Have you gotten to the point where you're almost tired of praying about the same thing?

What happens to our minds, wills, and emotions when answers don't come when we think they will?

What happens if our "due season" of answered prayer doesn't come for an entire decade? How do we respond when our prayers aren't answered in ways we expected?

How do we navigate seeing someone else receive their answer while we're still waiting?

Often, in the pain of unanswered prayer, we ask, "Is God truly good? And if He is good, why do my prayers for good, God-glorifying things go unanswered?"

When we stop thinking God's plan and perfect will for our lives are good, we play into the age-old challenge that began in the garden of Eden. God gave Adam and Eve the freedom to eat from any tree in the garden except the tree of the knowledge of good and evil. The consequence of eating from that tree was death. But then the cunning serpent asked Eve, "Did God really say, 'You can't eat from any tree in the garden'?" (Gen. 3:1).

At that very moment, Eve began questioning God's goodness by disobeying His instructions. She took the fruit from the tree, shared it with Adam, who was right there with her, and they both ate. Dr. Tony Evans invites us to notice Satan's tactics in his Bible commentary. He "intentionally misrepresented God, implying that God had commanded, 'You can't eat from any tree in the garden.' One of Satan's oldest lies, as alluring today as then, is this: *God is holding out on you.*"[1]

Isn't that how we feel when prayers are unanswered? We wonder if God is holding out on us. Because we don't have all the answers, we question if it's our past sins that keep us from receiving God's blessings. We sometimes wish we could control the outcome and even get ahead of things. If we're honest, this waiting place can be frustrating and difficult when we're doing everything we possibly can—and yet nothing seems to be happening.

∷

My reason for writing this book is simple. I want to give us space to be honest with God and ourselves. There is not one Christian on earth who hasn't experienced a not-yet-answered prayer and the waiting that comes with it. As we journey through Scripture together, our hope will remind us God is always there. One of His names is Immanuel, which means "God with us." He is with us in moments of suffering and joy, traversing with us both in wilderness and in flourishing—all for His glory and our good.

Together, we'll unpack the discouragement that happens when it appears others' prayers are being answered while we're still waiting. We'll lament our not-yet-unanswered prayers with hope and assurance in the God who knows all and created all. And maybe the prayer has been answered, and we are left wrestling with the challenges of why it was answered in a particular way. This book doesn't resolve the "why" prayers that may go delayed or unanswered. Instead, we'll focus on what to do when this happens and how to view God in light of this.

This book is not about suppressing your feelings and emotions to appear content. It's about truly experiencing contentment amid the waiting that comes with unanswered prayer.

It's learning how biblical lament, grief, joy, and hope can all live together in harmony.

It's about seeing God in all the moments of our lives—even when His answer seems to be a resounding no—and trusting His sovereignty with peace.

We will be encouraged by the Scriptures restoring and strengthening our faith in the One who holds all things together.

And together, we will work to be anchored by hope even when it seems as if our dreams have fallen apart.

Are you ready to dismantle everything you may have thought about why your prayers aren't answered? Are you ready to explore what we can do when prayers aren't answered the way we thought and how we relate to Him even while we wait for answers?

If the answer is yes, remember this isn't a how-to book but more of a how-to-get-through book. Get in a comfortable place and grab a cup of coffee or tea. We will pray, exhale, laugh, lament, cry . . . and even experience some joy together.

Leaning in to "Barren"

At the start of 2022, I experienced one of my first trips to the desert to attend a writers' retreat in Scottsdale, Arizona.

One of the first things I noticed was the retreat center's lack of vegetation, other than a few flowers and cactus plants. This was generally the landscape of Arizona. Nonetheless, something about the barrenness, the rocks, and the majestic mountains made this landscape beautiful. Arizona isn't the only spot with this type of terrain.

I think too of places like the Red Rock Canyons just outside Las Vegas. For miles and miles, not much is to be seen but red rocks with very little vegetation. Still, people from all over the globe come to visit to hike, climb, bike, and explore.

The Bonneville Salt Flats in Utah have a similar beauty. The state website says, "Imagine a place so flat you seem to see the curvature of the planet, so barren not even the simplest life forms can exist."[2] This also is a destination that attracts life from all over the globe, enthusiastic visitors in awe of God's barren creation.

Desolate, Lacking in Charm ... and Beautiful?

The word *barren* can mean not productive, desolate, fruitless, devoid, lacking interest or charm, or lacking inspiration or ideas.[3]

This chapter is about that place during prayer where you feel like you are in a deserted, barren land with no relief, no water, no vegetation in sight. You are in the canyons and yet you can't see the beauty in it, can't see a way out, and in fact, you feel stifled.

You have prayed. You have even fasted. You have put the prayer on the altar and shared the prayer with people in your small group. You have talked and prayed about it with your spouse, your mentors, your friends.

Everyone in your immediate sphere of influence knows the prayer of your heart. And yet it seems like God is silent. Perhaps you are grappling with a reality or a direction you suddenly find yourself in that was not a part of your plan. The psalmist cries out that weeping may stay overnight, but joy comes in the morning (Ps. 30:5). You may still find yourself weeping for nights on end as you struggle to find your joy. As isolating as these moments may seem, you are not alone.

If God is all-powerful, why would He withhold good things?

What have you struggled with? What is your wasteland, that barren place, that's "fruitless," "devoid," "lacking inspiration or ideas"? Maybe it's something that has just lately come up. Maybe it's something you've wrestled with and prayed about for years. Maybe you're asking for complete healing from a hard diagnosis; maybe you seek to restore a friendship or see a child come to the Lord. For me, I had years of literal barrenness as I struggled through miscarriages and infertility.

Whatever it is for you, barrenness—a lack of fruitfulness in a particular area of life—is hard.

Perhaps well-meaning people have told you not to fret, that God is sovereign. Maybe you can relate with wrestling with the understanding that God is sovereign. This means God is ultimately the One in control and can do whatever He wants, however He wants. We still find ourselves asking, *If God is all-powerful, all-knowing, with all wisdom, why would He withhold good things?*

In 2021, my mother was diagnosed with metastatic breast cancer and now, at the time of this writing, is experiencing some complications. I did what most people would do when learning something like this. I prayed. Then I went to Google. Big mistake, going to Google.

I found myself going down a rabbit hole of reports and studies only to consistently see these words: "There is no known cure." Over the years, radiation and chemotherapy treatments would yield little fruit, only keeping my mother "stable." Our prayers remain steadfast; we know God can completely heal my mother. He is God and He has proven Himself throughout Scripture and in the lives of people all around us. Yet this place feels desolate, at times isolating, and hard. As we wait for God to answer, researching and trying treatment after treatment, it indeed feels as if we are in a barren land. When we think of the word *barrenness*, beauty is not what comes to mind.

> :: **TAKE A MOMENT**
>
> What situation in your life are you thinking of when you hear the word "barren"? Can there be any beauty in barrenness?

Erin is a forty-one-year-old woman working to piece her life back together after spending the last decade caregiving. She assisted her mother with taking care of her father who came home on hospice after a nine-year battle with cancer. The same week, her mother was diagnosed with frontotemporal dementia and Parkinson's disease.

In just a few years, Erin was thrust into full-time caregiving of both parents and soon would have to face the loss of both. She often grieves what her life has not been, her unmet hopes and expectations.

Erin is a single woman who desires a family of her own. Yet she has found herself navigating an incredibly difficult journey that feels anything but beautiful.

Seeing the need for caregivers to have community, Erin birthed

Next Gen Caregivers. She provides resources to help caregivers with burnout but has also become a beacon of light and encouragement for others who find themselves in similar situations.

At times, without the presence of her parents, Erin has felt like an orphan. But her loss has pushed her into depending on the Lord like never before. The care of her heavenly Father reminds her of John 14:18: "I will not leave you as orphans; I am coming to you." Through her work, Erin lifts the hands of other caregivers and reminds them of this truth. They are not alone.

Below the Surface

Perhaps, when we hear the word "barren," we can begin to think of what's possible—prayerfully using holy imagination—instead of remaining stuck on what only seems bleak. Maybe there are ways we can see God while in a barren, desolate state when it seems as though we are producing no fruit for the world to see and glorify God through our life. Could our barrenness be seasonal? Or if barrenness in a particular area of our lives is God's will, how do we make peace with that to live fully? Typically, men and women who experience a season that feels barren do whatever it takes to move out of it.

> *Beneath the surface of our lives, God is moving, preparing, sharpening, developing, stretching, and loving us while we wait.*

But how do we cope—how do we continue to remain faithful—when days and months turn into years, and we see little evidence of God moving in our circumstances?

I have an orchid in my kitchen. This plant requires little water, but most of the year it's dry, with not so much as a flower bud. It seems like it takes forever for a bud to finally appear, and then after a full year, we finally get to see it bloom. Then the orchid looks glorious—but the process to get there feels pretty boring, because it seems like nothing is happening.

But something is always happening beneath the surface. Beneath the surface of our lives, God is moving, preparing, sharpening, developing, stretching, and loving us while we wait.

How often do we seek to take things in our own hands when waiting on God becomes unbearable?

There are times when the Holy Spirit will lead us in what to do *while* we wait.

What have we done in desperation when waiting for an answer from God? In my own desperation from experiencing unexplained infertility, there were times I questioned if I married the right spouse. I have an amazing husband, but my mind would wander in these moments to wonder if I was in the right marriage.

While waiting for God to answer prayer, if we aren't careful, the enemy of this world can lead us into a rabbit hole of thoughts and ideas that do not come from God. When these thoughts come, we have a responsibility to take them captive, casting them down and replacing them with God's Word (see 2 Cor. 10:5). Seasons of barrenness—desolation or wasteland or disappointment—can often be filled with spiritual warfare of the mind. When we understand we have weapons of warfare through the armor of Christ, we are strengthened to walk through these hard times.

God Who Sees

Hagar was in a precarious situation. The slave of Abram's wife, Sarai, she had been given to Abram as his concubine and was now pregnant with his child. Even though the arrangement had been

Sarai's idea in the first place, Sarai's jealousy and anger caused her to mistreat Hagar so badly that the young woman ran away into the wilderness.

But she wasn't alone in that desolate place. In Genesis 16, we learn that an angel of the Lord spoke to her and assured her, "The LORD has heard your cry of affliction." Hagar was comforted and said, "You are El-Roi," which means "God sees me" (vv. 11, 13).

This is good news. This is the beauty of the gospel. He sees us, even when we are blind. He looks for us during the moments we hide and run. He lovingly calls us while we are in our most ungodly state, graciously inviting us to come to the realization that His Son, Jesus, died for our sins. God gives us an opportunity at life everlasting . . . displaying His grace to us over and over again until the day we meet Him.

> *For while we were still helpless, at the right time, Christ died for the ungodly. For rarely will someone die for a just person—though for a good person perhaps someone might even dare to die. But God proves his own love for us in that while we were still sinners, Christ died for us.* (ROM. 5:6–8)

:: **TAKE A MOMENT**
> Have you been in a place, like Hagar, where the suffering you've experienced feels like too much? Has this thought ever crossed your mind: "Does God see me?"

If your answer to these questions is yes, you are in the right place and reading the right book. We all have been in situations we didn't ask for and have sought our own measure of refuge and peace in the midst of them. There are seasons of life where we find ourselves desperately seeking answers to our prayers. There are also times where we are in cycles of suffering that are beyond our control.

I too have been the person who sees the prayers of others being answered around me, yet I was still waiting for God to move on my behalf. In many areas of my life, I am still in that place.

So what might God be inviting us to see and explore during these times of barrenness? Wherever we find ourselves, we must remember: God sees us and is with us. It's even one of His names:

> *See, the virgin will become pregnant*
> *and give birth to a son,*
> *and they will name him Immanuel.* (MATT. 1:23)

If you are like me, you have heard these words repeatedly throughout your life, to the point that they may sound cliché and just roll past you. But "they will name him Immanuel" and "God with us" are anything but clichés. The name of the One who came to seek and save the lost is a declaration and a reminder that He is with us.

Yet the truth is, God being with us doesn't always come with a feeling. There will be times we cannot "feel" His presence.

"God with us" won't always come with the chills and goosebumps you may get during a powerful worship song, or when you are on the brink of tears from singing a hymn that hits your soul.

"God with us" isn't always the feeling that pricks your heart when hearing a sermon that resonates with you.

"God with us" isn't just in those déjà vu moments where the Spirit of God reminds you of a dream you had that you are now living in.

"God with us" isn't just reflected in the moments we receive encouraging words from someone that only God Himself could have known we needed.

Although God *is* with us during all of those moments.

He is with us when we get the diagnosis in the doctor's office that shakes us to our core. He is with us when we get the news that a close relative has passed away. He is with us when we are rejected for a role we really wanted. He is with us during the deepest grief we ever experienced.

He is with us when our dreams are falling apart.

We must know that He is also with us in the stillness. He is with us in the silence. He is with us in our solitude, and in the moments where we don't have answers. He is with us during the highest of highs and the lowest of lows. It's because of His steadfast love that He walks with us through every trial, every season, and every moment. We see a continual thread of that love as He walks with countless women and men throughout Scripture.

Do you believe this? Can you come to the place where you believe this? Can you say with Hagar, "He is the God who sees me"?

Setting Our Minds Above

Set your minds on things above, not on earthly things.
(COL. 3:2)

One winter, we experienced a snow squall. A snow squall is a dangerous, sudden whiteout of snow that passes through an area. If you are driving when one hits, you'd want to pull over and wait it out because there is absolutely no visibility around you; all you see is the sudden snowstorm. What's interesting about these unique weather systems is they tend to clear up and move out quickly. Shortly after that day's snow squall passed, the sun came out.

Setting our minds on things above and not on earthly things requires us to know that just beyond whatever storm we are in, there is sun. There is light on the other side of darkness. This isn't just for weather systems but for our life here on earth. Our perspective must shift as we endeavor to see things that are just beyond. Just beyond what we see in front of us lies an eternal perspective that will sustain us if we grab hold of the truth of who God is.

We are going to walk through difficult, gut-wrenching things in this life. Things that we don't understand, that make us weep and boil with anger. And if you have lived at least twenty years or beyond, chances are you've already experienced heartbreak at some level.

As we walk together through the following chapters, we'll discover who God is in all of this while clinging to Him as our faith is tested.

He is not a Sovereign Spectator merely watching us go through all that we experience from His throne. Instead, He is a Sovereign Father, holding the hands of His children as we walk through valleys, shadows, wilderness, and barren lands.

These chapters are not filled with toxic positivity where you're motivated to just get over it, pull yourself up by your bootstraps, and simply dream a new dream. There is space here for you to lament the fact that you are still waiting after many years. This is a safe space for you to acknowledge that your dream fell apart or that maybe you didn't like the answer you received to a heartfelt prayer. We may cry in this place, but we will also dry our tears and rejoice, knowing the goodness of God is present in barren places.

God sees you and has not forgotten. May our hearts be open to receive what He's doing even when we don't understand.

⁝⁝ TAKE A MOMENT

How have you seen the Lord work in moments of suffering? What aspects of God's character have you experienced in action? Let's take a moment to pray and thank the Lord for His character.

Father, thank You for the gift of Your Son, Jesus, who redeems us from our sin. I thank You for never leaving or forsaking me. Lord, help me see You as I wait, pray, and continue to trust You to answer the prayers of my heart. Help me trust Your will and use my story for Your glory. In Jesus' name, Amen.

2

Lament

> *Let the globe, if nothing else, say this is true.*
> *That even as we grieved, we grew.*
> *That even as we hurt, we hoped.*
> *That even as we tired, we tried.*
> *That we'll forever be tied together, victorious.*
> —Amanda Gorman, "The Hill We Climb"[1]

MY FIRST EXPERIENCE WITH SORROW that I remember was when my dad suddenly wasn't in the home.

I remember drawing a picture with him pulling out in his car; I wanted him to return. At the time, my mother had put him out because he took money from our household income and used it to buy drugs. This money had been for our school clothes and now we had nothing.

My mother had every right to kick him out of the house at that time, but my young mind could not comprehend what was happening or why. I couldn't imagine the sorrow my mother was experiencing watching the love of her life destroy his life through drug usage. All I wanted was my daddy back home.

Eventually the winter came, and my mother couldn't let him be homeless. So despite the challenges my dad's drug addiction would bring the family for years to come, she felt he would be better off at home with us. If he were living in the streets, my mother believed he would not live long.

Yet as I grew and came into the knowledge of what my father struggled with, it would bring a different kind of sorrow. This sorrow was often coupled with anger during my teen and young adult years. As I grew older and a little wiser, I took time to learn more of my father's story. I also learned more about forgiveness and how a just God has forgiven me.

A Language of Hope

> *Be kind and compassionate to one another, forgiving one another, just as God also forgave you in Christ.* (EPH. 4:32)

I titled this chapter "Lament," which sounds like a sad word . . . well, it is. But when we understand lament in the biblical sense, we can learn to lament in a way that is healthy and gives us hope.

Let me tell you more about my family's story.

The gospel changing my life and giving me the ultimate hope is what shifted my sorrow over my father to lament. The anger and sorrow I had over my father for years became a lament that I would have until the day he went to be with the Lord.

My father joined the United States Marine Corps when he was seventeen. Vietnam was beginning its cleanup, and my father was a part of Operation Frequent Wind. This operation required my father to do things that he did not want to talk about. I am sure my father wrestled with PTSD, though that term wasn't used at the time.

Then in the 1980s, Washington, DC, like many cities, became

ravaged by the crack epidemic. As crack flooded our communities, my father, seeking to numb his own pain and mental anguish, became a continual user.

I don't know everything my father experienced in life. I know that in 2015, as my father came out of yet another overdose with the assistance of Narcan administered by paramedics, I told him I wanted him to live. I wanted him to fight. He didn't say a word but cried in my arms, and we grieved together. He wanted to have hope that he could kick the addiction. There were times he would ask for prayer even during his darkest days.

In those moments, we began to understand the language of lament.

"Yet I Have Hope"

Over time I joined groups that taught me more about addiction and learned that this was a sickness. I became committed to forgiving my father and, along with my mother and brother, worked through what it was like to love someone who wrestled with addiction. He would have stints where he would go without using for weeks or months at a time. And then, loneliness or depression would seep in, a phone call would happen, and he would be back at square one.

Over the years, my father would be in and out of rehab and have months where he would fight his addiction by going cold turkey and pushing through the withdrawals. He did this for my wedding in 2011. I told him that I refused to have him walk me down the aisle if he was high. And so, he did what he needed to do. On September 24, 2011, he walked me down the aisle, head held up, proud, and drug free.

But his addiction remained a struggle for him.

In the months prior to his passing, he was drug free. My parents came over to spend the night at our brand-new home to celebrate my mom's birthday. We all went out to dinner, and my brother and sister-in-law disclosed the news that they were pregnant. We rejoiced! This would be the first grandchild.

In the days following that great news, my parents joined us for a surprise celebration for my husband's birthday. The next day, we all went to church together. I remember seeing my father go up for prayer. I always wondered what he asked them to pray about, but my heart was at peace, watching my dad—who once didn't have a desire to even attend church—engaged in the service and praying. I had consistently prayed over the years for God to heal my dad from his addiction. This was one of the seasons where it seemed as if we were living in an answered prayer.

After service, I invited my parents to brunch, but my father wanted to go home. He said he was tired, and I believed him; he carried a small oxygen tank on his shoulder, the simple task of breathing becoming more difficult as the complications of Chronic Obstructive Pulmonary Disease (COPD) grew.

Two days later, I received the call that my father had passed away from the challenges of COPD. It was September 5, 2017. As he struggled with breathing that afternoon, instead of calling the paramedics, he simply asked my mother to pray. As she prayed, he transitioned from this world to the next. Upon hearing the news, I wailed. I had never felt a pain so deep. My earthly father was gone, and though it brought comfort that our last encounter was at church together, the hole that this loss brought was like nothing I'd ever known.

My father, Gregory Schumpert, was one of my best friends in the world. He was the greatest cook and a comedian in his own right. When he walked into a room, he was the life of the party. A friend to any and everyone, he was the type of person who never met a stranger. This kindhearted man was also our protector, our fixer-upper, gardener, and mechanic. It seemed as if he knew a little something about everything. He was not his addiction.

I lament over his life and his constant fight to be free from addiction.

I lament that he did not get to meet his grandchildren.

I lament that he didn't get to experience complete healing on this earth. Yet I have hope.

Weeks before he passed, he had received Jesus Christ, and our family saw the fruit of that decision in his life. Although addiction was a stronghold he would wrestle with until his final days, it did not keep him from the hands of our Lord. His addiction eventually drew him to his knees. The love and grace poured upon him from family allowed him to see Christ on earth. Even through my father's pain, God had a plan to save.

> **TAKE A MOMENT**
>
> Can you remember your first experience with sorrow or grief? How did it change you? Today, are there ways you are able to see the character of God through that experience?

What Is Biblical Lament?

Mark Vroegop writes, "Each step of lament is part of a pathway toward hope. In the address, the heart is turned to God in prayer. Complaint clearly and bluntly lays out the reasons behind the sorrow. From there the lamenter usually makes a request for God to act—to do something. Finally, nearly every lament ends with renewed trust and praise."[2]

Biblical lament is an expression of sorrow and grief that gives us room to be honest with what we are feeling before God. It incorporates specific elements that allow us to cultivate hope within our grief. All throughout Scripture we find examples of lament. We see David lament over his sin in the Psalms. We also see Jeremiah lament over the children of Judah in Lamentations, to the extent that he became known as "the Weeping Prophet."

Biblical lament takes our sorrows to a place that is fortified in the knowledge of God. It is a prayer either spoken aloud or silent, which lays out every burden and care before the Lord. Laments are raw and honest communication on behalf of oneself or someone else. Lament may be personal or communal. I have come to appreciate prayers of lament like the one found in Psalm 22. David knew the healing power of lament, and in this psalm, he goes from suffering to praise.

> *My God, my God, why have you abandoned me?*
> *Why are you so far from my deliverance*
> *and from my words of groaning?*
> *My God, I cry by day, but you do not answer,*
> *by night, yet I have no rest.*
> *But you are holy,*
> *enthroned on the praises of Israel.*
> *Our ancestors trusted in you;*
> *they trusted, and you rescued them.*
> *They cried to you and were set free;*
> *they trusted in you and were not disgraced.* (PS. 22:1–5)

Why Is This Happening?

As a child, I remember hearing that I should "never question God." Yet there are times when great heartbreaks and deep pain will produce many questions. We see in Psalm 22 that we are in good company. Throughout Psalms and Lamentations, we witness how David and Jeremiah grapple with hard questions through their prayers. We serve a God who is in touch with our emotions, understands suffering, and can handle our questions.

The words of David in Psalm 22:1, "My God, my God, why have you abandoned me?" mirror the words of Jesus in Matthew 27:46: "About three in the afternoon Jesus cried out with a loud voice, 'Elí, Elí, lemá sabachtháni?' that is, 'My God, my God, why have you abandoned me?'"

If Christ, the Son of God—the One who took on all the suffering of the world and died on the cross for our sins—had questions in His deepest moments of lament, how much more will we? There will come a time when our question of why this is happening may turn into *What am I supposed to do or learn in this?* Biblical lament doesn't rush to a solution. True lament leans into the questions of our heart, bringing them to an omniscient, all-knowing God.

In lament we have space to grieve; to bring all the pain we are experiencing and working through to our Father's feet. Yet as we grieve, as we question, as we wrestle, biblical lament will always bring us to a point of acknowledgment of who God is. In Psalm 22:3, in the midst of suffering, David comes to a point of contention where he extols the name of God, "But you are holy, enthroned on the praises of Israel." We see similarities in Lamentations 3:17–20:

> *In lament we have space to grieve; to bring all the pain we are experiencing and working through to our Father's feet.*

> *I have been deprived of peace;*
> *I have forgotten what prosperity is.*
> *Then I thought, "My future is lost,*
> *as well as my hope from the* Lord.*"*
>
> *Remember my affliction and my homelessness,*
> *the wormwood and the poison.*
> *I continually remember them*
> *and have become depressed.*

In Lamentations 3:17–21, Jeremiah doesn't mince words. He states what he is feeling and experiencing at this moment. He has been deprived of peace; he has forgotten what prosperity is. He experiences negative thoughts about his future, and as he thinks about his past and all that he's been through, he becomes depressed.

Oh, how relatable are these words from Jeremiah! At the moment, it seems as if Jeremiah would benefit from trauma therapy, if it were available. However, in the middle of his lament there is a turning point in verse 21 as he states, "yet I call this to mind." For him to call something to mind in order to experience hope means that Jeremiah had to have known it beforehand. In this moment of despair, he pulled on what he knew would always be true: God's faithfulness.

> *Yet I call this to mind,*
> *and therefore I have hope.*
> *Because of the* Lord's *faithful love*
> *we do not perish,*
> *for his mercies never end.*
> *They are new every morning;*
> *great is your faithfulness!* (vv. 21–23)

F. B. Huey, in the New American Commentary, shares that "the basis for renewed hope is God's 'great love.'"[3] For those of us in Christ, we understand that His great love has been displayed in His sacrifice for our sin. A God who loves us so much that He would take on the sins of the world surely is with us in the darkest moments of our lives. This is the steadfast love that ultimately gives those who know Him hope anchored in truth.

Warfare in Lament

In lament, there are moments where we must take note of the spiritual warfare we may be in. Any time our thoughts begin to go against the knowledge of who God is and His character, we must work to take these thoughts captive. It is much easier to allow ourselves to go down a dark path and sink into a depression about what we are experiencing. It takes conscious effort to cast down thoughts that do not come from God and lean into what we know is true about Him. Paul speaks about this in 2 Corinthians 10:3–5:

> For although we live in the flesh, we do not wage war according to the flesh, since the weapons of our warfare are not of the flesh, but are powerful through God for the demolition of strongholds. We demolish arguments and every proud thing that is raised up against the knowledge of God, and we take every thought captive to obey Christ. (2 COR. 10:3–5)

During seasons of lament, we must come to a point where we are taking our thoughts captive to make them obey Christ. To make a thought obey Christ simply means our thoughts line up with the truth of Scripture. What types of thoughts would fall into this category of needing to be taken captive?

Maybe it's self-deprecating thoughts that would seek to tear you down further than what you are already experiencing. Or maybe your thoughts are leading you into a place of questioning the divinity of Christ, His ultimate power, or His love for you.

If these are the types of thoughts we are having in our lament, we must come to the place where we are actively taking these thoughts captive to obey Christ. This means we are replacing the misguided thoughts with the truth of Scripture.

> *The enemy of this world seeks to draw us into these things for instantaneous comfort, instead of sitting and dealing with our grief in a healthy way.*

In order to do this effectively, we must have a healthy theology of suffering. The enemy of our souls knows that we are most vulnerable when we are sad. This is how so many of us find ourselves using unhealthy coping mechanisms—such as substance or alcohol abuse, overworking, or mindlessly scrolling online. Our enemy seeks to draw us into these things for superficial yet instantaneous comfort, instead of sitting and dealing with our grief in a healthy way.

Leaning into Lament

We live in a world that chases good vibes and good times, so leaning into lament may feel uncomfortable and even unnatural. Sometimes our society acknowledges collective hardship—such as a tragedy in a community or a national event like 9/11—with a moment of silence at an event, and then we move on. Comedians on late-night talk shows attempt to make us feel lighter by telling jokes about difficult issues in the news.

Lament

These ways of coping aren't inherently wrong when included in the full spectrum of our healing. Who doesn't need an escape from the trials of this world? Laughter is often necessary for our healing—and so is lamenting. We miss a huge step in healing when we don't lean into our opportunity to lament as a community and as individuals. Here are some things to know about practically leaning into lament:

Have Your Moment and Cry Out

After my father passed, there were moments when I would try to be strong for those around me. I was planning his celebration of life service, and I didn't feel as though I really had time to grieve or indulge in tears. But there came a time when I could not hold back any longer. So I allowed myself to have that moment.

I was patient with myself as I went through all the various stages of grief over time. I lamented as I cooked foods that he loved that we would no longer enjoy together. I wept as certain songs came on the radio. I grieved over all the holidays we would no longer share. I allowed my eyes to fill with tears when I drove past my parents' old condo. I cried out to God, bringing all frustration, anxiety, sadness, and anger to His feet. I grieved, I cried out, I prayed through tears, I asked questions, I journaled, and I lamented my father's departure from earth.

And during those moments, I often felt the presence of the Lord right with me. We may not always know the answers that brought us to a particular place, but we can trust that Christ is with us in each moment.

> *You yourself have recorded my wanderings.*
> *Put my tears in your bottle.*
> *Are they not in your book?* (PS. 56:8)

Affirm or Reaffirm Your Trust

Take some time to affirm your trust in who God is, His Word, and His character. It is human to wrestle with this part, but it is the part of lament that brings us into restoration. Oftentimes, we are never quite the same after experiencing whatever brought us into lament. We are new creatures who are acquainted with grief. Yet we have hope. It is this practice of affirming or in some cases reaffirming our trust in Christ that brings us into hope.

This is our Lamentations 3:21 "yet I call this to mind" moment. I found myself instinctively doing this the day I learned of my father's passing. During one of the deepest pains of my life, I began to affirm who God is to our family—that although it hurt like nothing we had ever experienced, we could trust that our father is healed and whole in the presence of the Lord. When you are ready, take time to affirm your trust in the Lord verbally and/or in writing. I will not promise you that the burden will immediately lift. But redirecting our attention to the One who sees and knows all is a great start for our healing.

Make Your Requests Known

In Philippians 4, though he is in prison, Paul is encouraging the church of Philippi, which is facing opposition. As they are experiencing worry, he tells them something important about peace:

> *Don't worry about anything, but in everything, through prayer and petition with thanksgiving, present your requests to God. And the peace of God, which surpasses all understanding, will guard your hearts and minds in Christ Jesus.* (PHIL. 4:6–7)

Paul tells them that through prayer and petition with thanksgiving to bring every request to God. And *then* the peace of God, which is beyond our own understanding, will anchor our hearts and minds in Christ. Oftentimes during some of our deepest heartbreaks we forget to pause and simply petition.

I've had times when I have asked the Lord to take away the sting of what I am feeling, to help me walk through it, and to give me supernatural strength to endure. Whatever it is that we are walking through that brings us to a place of lament, it's important to know that God still cares about our desires and needs. Nothing is too big or small of a request. Bring it all to Him.

The Duality of Joy and Lament

Have you ever been in the middle of grief and a thought came that made you smile or laugh? The day we buried my father I had concert tickets to see one of my favorite performers. As family and friends were helping clean up our home after the repast, they asked if I was still going. "Of course not!" I exclaimed. I was surprised they even asked me that. Why would I go to a concert on the day we buried my father?

But my family insisted that I go. Besides, my father had been a music lover and would have appreciated knowing I was having a good time. However, I thought, this was my season for lamenting. How could I go somewhere and do something that would bring me joy during such a heavy time? Despite my initial feelings, I decided to go. To my surprise, my husband and I had the most amazing time. I sang and rapped my little heart out. And for a while, the heaviness of the moment left me.

Was I still grieving? Yes.

Was I experiencing joy? Absolutely.

Grief is complicated like that at times. We may have moments during a season of lament that bring us joy. It may not be a concert, but it could be as simple as a thought that brings laughter or a smile to our face. When I returned home after the concert, I remember feeling a bit of guilt for having had such a good time during such a difficult season in my life. I love the way Dr. John Onwuchekwa speaks about this duality using the metaphor of coffee: "Coffee, like life, is about receiving the bitterness and the sweetness together."[4]

Yes, grief is bitter and lamenting is hard. But we'll find moments of sweetness that we experience during our seasons of lament. So there is no reason to feel guilty when you experience joy during lament. Embrace them both, as they are both a part of the process.

My friend Sethlina experienced the passing of her sweet boy Shiloh, who died from complications related to a long and arduous fight with sickle cell anemia.

The day Shiloh took his last breath, the family was preparing to travel to celebrate his older brother's birthday. Sethlina made one of the most difficult decisions of her life in that very moment. She chose to go ahead with plans to spend the weekend with her other two children, moving forward with a birthday celebration at Great Wolf Lodge.

I am sure that despite their tears of sorrow over Shiloh's loss, Sethnlina also smiled to see her other children enjoying the massive water park at the lodge, though keenly missing their youngest brother who would have been following along.

After the loss of her son, I've continued to witness Sethlina walk in the duality of joy and lament that life often brings us. In honor of Shiloh, she has created a beautiful garden of luscious fruits, flourishing vegetables, and gorgeous flowers, most of which she planted by seed. We speak about the joy this garden brings her while she will forever navigate the incomparable loss of a son. And every year as she joyfully celebrates the birthday of her son Levi, she also remembers and laments Shiloh who had transitioned to glory the day before.

This is what it looks like to walk in this duality; it is the true definition of bittersweet.

Shiloh's journey brought people together all over the world in prayer for what we knew God could do. He chose to heal him completely on the other side of heaven. And although we don't understand it, we know that Shiloh is very much alive and present with the Lord. In fact, we are confident, and we would prefer to be away from the body and at home with the Lord (2 Cor. 5:8).

Offer Praise to God

This may feel like the last thing you want to do, yet it's our praise that lifts us out of the darkness of our grief. Praise helps us see the light through our tears as we worship. C. S. Lewis stated, "No one ever told me that grief felt so like fear. I am not afraid, but the sensation is like being afraid. The same fluttering in the stomach, the same restlessness, the yawning. I keep on swallowing. At other times it feels like being mildly drunk or concussed."[5]

Grief can definitely take us places within our mind and body.

The way sadness impacts our nervous system is real and often feels like a roller coaster you desperately want to end. And although grief is a process and something that we carry with us through various stages, offering praises to the Lord while grieving serves as a stabilizer.

Our lives are full of wilderness and valley moments.

When feelings of grief, anxiety, and fear flood our hearts, our praise acts like a pacemaker, stabilizing our hearts and keeping us focused on the only one who can heal us. Acknowledging the

Lord's goodness through praise shifts us into the Lamentations 3:21 "call to mind" moment. We praise Him because He's God, not simply because of the good gifts He's given us.

> *Then Moses and the Israelites sang this song to the* LORD.
> *They said:*
> *I will sing to the* LORD,
> *for he is highly exalted;*
> *he has thrown the horse*
> *and its rider into the sea.*
> *The* LORD *is my strength and my song;*
> *he has become my salvation.*
> *This is my God, and I will praise him,*
> *my father's God, and I will exalt him.*
> *The* LORD *is a warrior;*
> *the* LORD *is his name.* (EX. 15:1–3)

This expression of praise is modeled by Moses and the Israelites who were brought out of captivity into the wilderness. Our lives are full of wilderness and valley moments. Moments that are difficult and moments that may cause suffering and great pain. Yet we can make the decision to praise our way through pain with the understanding that this pain will not remain.

Jesus reminds us of this in the words He shares with His disciples: "I have told you these things so that in me you may have peace. You will have suffering in this world. Be courageous! I have conquered the world" (John 16:33). What does this mean to us during our lament? It means that we can rest knowing that pain and suffering are ultimately conquered by Christ. He has defeated and overcome all of the consequences of sin, death, and the enemy of this world, Satan. And even through deepest grief we can choose to praise Him because we know the end of the story found in Revelation 21:3–4:

> Then I heard a loud voice from the throne: Look, God's dwelling is with humanity, and he will live with them. They will be his peoples, and God himself will be with them and will be their God. He will wipe away every tear from their eyes. Death will be no more; grief, crying, and pain will be no more, because the previous things have passed away.

Lament with Hope

Believers lament with hope because we know that our lives don't merely end here. For all eternity, Christ will dwell with human beings and will remove every situation that would have brought lament during our earthly lives. This is a reason to offer great praise!

As we posture our hearts to offer praise, we gain strength from the One who brings us through. Some of my sweetest times with the Lord were spent crying out in praise, prayer, and worship before Him during my lowest points of lament. Leaning into lament is what gives us beauty for ashes. We are honest with ourselves and with the Lord, opening our hearts to be comforted by the Holy Spirit. Lament helps us process grief in a healthy way instead of bottling it up and allowing bitterness to build. When we lean into lament, we declare that we are not alone, and we rest in the hands of Christ who carries our burdens. This is how healing begins.

TAKE A MOMENT

Use the steps found in this section and write out your own lament:

- What do you need from the Lord? Cry out to the Lord and use this moment to pour out any heartache, any questions you have wrestled with, or any complaint.
- Take some time to affirm your trust in Christ. This is your "call to mind" moment. Think about all the ways God has come through in your life. Think about the times you didn't know how you would get through a certain moment. Journal what you know about God's character through what you have experienced outside of this moment and within this moment of lament.
- What is the thing you desire the most? Write that down and don't be ashamed of what you need. Petition the Lord with thanksgiving.
- Offer praises and assurance to the Lord. Why will you and why do you praise Him?

3

Exile

I INITIALLY WRESTLED WITH A title for this chapter. Millions of people in our world today are on the move—some in search of a better life, others displaced because of war, countless people unable to feed their families due to famine or other natural occurrences, some sent adrift by religious persecution, others forcibly removed from their homes for myriad reasons.

Most of us might consider "exiles" to be other people, not us; though as we'll examine in this chapter, just by being a Christian in this world, we're in a type of exile. And when we find our dreams falling apart, we may go through times where we feel displaced.

Exiles Under the Old Covenant

Let's start by looking at times of historic exile as recounted in the Bible.

In Scripture, the people of God, i.e., the kingdoms of Israel and Judah, experienced two major exilic periods. The first is the Assyrian exile or captivity, which began around 740 BC when King Pul of Assyria "took the Reubenites, Gadites, and half the tribe of Manasseh into exile" (1 Chron. 5:26). People were taken from the homes, from their nation, from all that was familiar, and forced to relocate to a foreign country. About twenty years later, the capital city of Israel, Samaria, was overtaken. The second exile is the Babylonian exile, which began under King Nebuchadnezzar in 608 BC. By 586 BC, Jerusalem was in ruins.[1]

We read about these exiles and the impact on the people of God throughout various historical, prophetic, and poetic books of the Bible. These periods of exile were a form of judgment due to the sin of God's people. Despite being witnesses to God's power as He led them out of slavery in Egypt through the wilderness by His sovereign hand and into the promised land, and despite these accounts being passed down through generations, the people of God continued to raise up idols and worship false gods.

Throughout the Old Testament we see the cycle of sin where God's people would repent and agree to turn from their wicked ways. But they would soon return to their same habits, and then judgment would be brought upon them through military defeats and constant warfare with surrounding nations. After hundreds of years of this cycle, God finally allowed His people to be exiled or held in captivity due to the gravity of their sin and forced to leave the land He had promised them.

Exiles are devastating, and the people who experience such things are never the same. In many cases, people banished from their homeland lose contact with family members; some don't live through the process. This displacement completely shifts the trajectory of their lives and the lives of their families. Its impact is often felt for generations to come.

Exiles of the New Covenant

Likely you have not lived through a drastic displacement as we are describing. But did you know that as a Christian living under the new covenant, you are an exile? For the Christian, we are all just sojourners through this earthly life because we are citizens of heaven, our forever home, and we are to live in light of that truth.

Peter encourages Christ followers to live as exiles by continuing to be set apart, abstaining from the sin in this world: "Dear friends, I urge you as strangers and exiles to abstain from sinful desires that wage war against the soul" (1 Peter 2:11).

And so, I wrestled with naming this chapter "exile" because of varied uses of that word: exiles in history, the displacement of millions in our own day, and the truth that under the new covenant, Christ followers are to live as exiles.

Still and all, there are times when people feel like they are in exile within their own communities. So we're going to examine another shade of meaning of "exile" now. For the purposes of this chapter, when I use the term *exile*, I am referring to the person who feels displaced or abandoned within the body of Christ.

Exiled During Life Change

The call to live as exiles is done within the community and the church. Yet there are moments when we feel exiled within this very group where we should feel at home.

This displacement is not a part of God's judgment on us. It is not due to our sin or something that we brought on ourselves. This displacement may or may not be from our personal choice. When we are in this particular place in our lives, it may feel stifling, uncomfortable, and depressing.

The type of displacement I am referring to is often inflicted by the body of Christ and among other believers. It may occur when there is a significant life change. Perhaps you are a woman in your thirties without children or a spouse. You slowly watch women around you getting married and suddenly you are not invited to the "wives" night out. Or maybe your friends begin to have children, and you are no longer called for the birthday parties or mommy dates. You do not fit in.

It is not wrong to gather with certain others. We all need community with people who share our life experiences. But when we begin to isolate ourselves into communities with people who only share similar life experiences and subconsciously push out or "exile" those whose season of life is different, we do ourselves and others a disservice. We've become too narrow. We're missing out on the beauty of fulfilling relationships.

I believe it's important to ask ourselves, *How do I walk with someone whose life has suddenly shifted?*

Suppose two children are very sick and need to spend extended time in the hospital. Their mothers become acquainted, and their relationship develops into a close friendship—they have a natural kinship due to their current situation. They spend time encouraging each other because they both can relate to having an immunocompromised child.

Then one mother's life takes a drastic turn as her daughter's condition suddenly worsens, and not long after, she passes away. The child of the other mother continues to improve and is able to leave the hospital and enjoy a typical childhood.

The mother of the healthy child has a choice. She can continue to move forward with her life and embrace the blessing of her child who continues to live. She can gradually lose contact with the other mom—because how could she possibly relate to this woman now? Or she can make the choice to walk with this mom through her suffering while also thanking the Lord for how He has kept her child. She can find ways to care for this mom and wrap her in love, connection, and support.

One decision centers around our personal comfort. It feels safe and it avoids any awkwardness. It doesn't require much work to slowly retreat, leaving the other person on their island of despair.

The other decision honors the second greatest commandment: "Love your neighbor as yourself. All the Law and the Prophets depend on these two commands" (Matt. 22:39–40).

This decision may be uncomfortable and is not always convenient. It requires us to be thoughtful, sacrificial, and prayerful about our conversations and interactions.

Exiled Due to Hesitance

As a part of the call to love our neighbors well, we must be cognizant of how we contribute to the feelings of exile those in our community experience. There are times we become so engrossed in our own worlds that we don't see those who are suffering within our midst. There are times this is not evident; people don't wear T-shirts emblazoned with "MY CHILD IS WAYWARD AND I'M LOSING FAITH." Our tendency as humans is to remain in our comfort zone, that place where we don't have to think of what to say, how to engage, and avoid all feelings of, well... discomfort.

You might remember when nine people were tragically shot to death at the Mother Emanuel AME church in Charleston, South Carolina, in 2015. At that time, I was a part of a multiethnic

> *Being the hands and feet of Christ requires us to see beyond ourselves and act.*

church. After hearing the news of this deplorable act of violence on African American congregants by a white male, many people of color who came to church that Sunday were devastated. We were grieving in a church where we were the minority. I thought, "Surely the pastor is going to acknowledge this event and will at least pause the normal flow of service to pray for those families directly impacted and those who are processing grief."

To our disappointment, the church service went on as usual with its usual worship, sermon, and a push for people to join groups. Meanwhile, many people in the church were experiencing fear, anger, distrust, and overall grief. I reached out to this pastor and learned that he was so concerned with saying the wrong thing that he didn't say anything at all. There are times throughout our lives where we all feel this way.

Instead of leaning into our comfort that avoids certain discussions, perhaps a better response would have been, "Hey, I'm concerned about saying the wrong thing, but I believe that it's necessary to acknowledge the pain of many in this room. We as a church are with you, we grieve with you, and together we will process this horrible tragedy." We are all deserving of simple compassion, especially in the house of the Lord. This is the place where part of being the hands and feet of Christ requires us to see beyond ourselves and act. If we are intentional in truly connecting, discipling, and building relationships with people, we learn their stories, we hear their pain, we walk with them. Here are three primary ways to walk alongside people who may be in a season of waiting or wrestling with the answer of *no* or *not yet*.

Exiled by Limited Hospitality

> *Hospitality is a sacred act through which we can reflect God's grace, love and heart in our own lives. In opening our homes*

and hearts to others, we not only "love our neighbors" but we honor Christ, who taught us that when we welcome a stranger, we welcome Him.² —Maaden Eshete Jones

Don't neglect to show hospitality, for by doing this so some have welcomed angels as guests without knowing it. (HEB. 13:2)

Be hospitable to one another without complaining. Just as each one has received a gift, use it to serve others, as good stewards of the varied grace of God. (1 PETER 4:9–10)

Hospitality is one way we may love our neighbors well and promote healing among one another, all while using our homes to glorify God. This is a practice that's often encouraged as a way to reach out to the nonbeliever. Many of our church programs will encourage small group study among people who have similar interests or are in the similar stages of life, such as singles groups or mom groups.

But what would it look like for us to practice hospitality by reaching across those boundary lines? If we did, married people could interact with and learn from singles. Singles can learn from parents and engage with families. Those with disabilities can interact with those without disabilities, and the older can interact with the younger.

Some of the most transformational and impactful experiences I've had have been breaking bread with my elders, or with a younger single woman. In both types of experiences there have been helpful exchanges in our conversations that have been restorative, especially as I walked through seasons of loss and suffering. We must never get to a place where we stop learning from one another. So when that sister who lost her baby or that brother whose wife recently died come across your mind, invite them to the table. These vulnerable moments are when people—believers and non-believers or lapsed believers—may be wrestling with their faith. Your invitation to the table and compassionate, radical hospitality could be the very thing that helps them see the goodness of God in the midst of uncertainty or heartbreak.

When extending hospitality, we must push past the need to be perfect. Your home may or may not be Instagram photo– or *Good Housekeeping* magazine–ready, and that is okay. Real homes are lived-in and welcoming. It's the love that fills the home and the people in it that make it meaningful. Some of my sweetest moments of hospitality were spent living in Washington, DC, as a single woman in my small two-bedroom, one-bathroom house. I would share my favorite snack, which has always been popcorn, and offer a cup of tea or coffee, and some fruit.

The conversations that have occurred in those simple moments of hospitality have been healing and memorable. What matters most is having a heart to serve and the presence you create by sharing the love of Christ to all who enter your home. As image bearers within the body of Christ, hospitality provides a way for us to engage and learn from one another, to support, pray, offer wisdom, or simply listen.

> :: **TAKE A MOMENT**
>
> Think about the person in your life who has recently experienced disappointment or is grappling with grief. Or does someone come to mind whose stage in life is different from yours? Perhaps you are a mom and you've noticed an older woman who always sits alone in church. Or you are a single woman and there is a college student you know who is living far from her home. Who could use an invitation to

your table? Pray for that person by name at this moment. And then make a conscious effort to connect and extend an invitation.

Exiled by Lack of Listening

Have you ever been in the middle of a conversation pouring your heart out, and then you ask the person you are sharing with a question, and they respond in a way that clearly shows they weren't listening? The exasperating feeling of not being heard is one that most of us have experienced at some point.

If we're honest, active listening is a skill that doesn't come naturally to most of us. For one thing, we have constant technological distractions around us. Many of us are so connected to our smartphones and smartwatches we look at them before we pay attention to the real human in front of us. Having these conveniences may often pull us away from active listening.

When we hear about people who are grieving or in any kind of pain, it may be a natural inclination to jump in, fix the problem, and save the day. I admit, I am that person who likes to fix things and situations and who has struggled with a "savior" complex. Oftentimes, when someone is sharing, I am already thinking about my response before they finish speaking.

Needless to say, a lack of active listening has not always fared me well in marriage. I became aware of the importance of active listening in a marriage counseling session. I am truly grateful to have developed this skill over time that not only helped me in marriage but in all of my relationships. This is a skill we must intentionally practice.

To listen actively means we are listening without forming an immediate response. This requires patience and humility, allowing the person speaking to share freely. We simply sit, giving the person our undivided attention while making eye contact and assuring them that we are listening through our body language. Again, resist the urge to glance at your phone during this time.

Then, prior to offering our feedback or a response, simply ask if they would like to hear our thoughts. This is also the time to ask questions for clarity if there is something you don't understand. When engaging in active listening, we are slow to speak. This type of listening centers on the person who is sharing, providing an environment where they feel heard and understood. Remember, when someone is hurting, suffering, or wrestling, the last thing they needed is to not feel heard after they have been vulnerable.

Last, as believers, this type of listening opens the door for opportunities to pray. Praying is a reminder that we do not have all the answers, and we can approach the One in prayer who does. It sets us in a place of submission and humility as we pray together through what we have discussed. It draws us closer as the community of saints, and it exalts Christ as the One who knows all.

> **TAKE A MOMENT**
>
> When was the last time you had a conversation and practiced active listening? What did you learn during that experience? If you haven't been practicing active listening, try to during your next conversation.

Exiles Together

> *Now the entire group of those who believed were of one heart and mind, and no one claimed that any of his possessions was his own, but instead they held everything in common. With*

> *great power the apostles were giving testimony to the resurrection of the Lord Jesus, and great grace was on all of them. For there was not a needy person among them because all those who owned lands or houses sold them, brought the proceeds of what was sold, and laid them at the apostles' feet. This was then distributed to each person as any had need.* (Acts 4:32–35)

Imagine being part of a church where you never felt as if you were on an island, displaced, or that you didn't belong. You are free to be vulnerable because it is modeled through the transparency of the members and leadership. In this church, we are aware of the unanswered prayers or individuals who are wrestling with answers they have received.

Our awareness moves us beyond empathy to compassion to practically meeting the needs of those around us. We know the name of the woman who just lost her baby, the husband who became a widower, the person who received a sobering prognosis, the family praying for their wayward son or daughter, the single who desires to be married, and the person who has been unemployed and praying for a new career door to open.

We know their names because this church has created a culture of vulnerability and transparency from the top down. These things are not shared for the sake of gossip (or gossip disguised as a prayer request), but for the church to come together to pray for the needs of those who are in these seasons of life, using our collective resources to meet those needs. Leadership in this church is intentional with getting to know the members, their testimonies, the things they are praying for, and what they are walking through.

I would imagine this is what the early church looked like in the book of Acts. I believe these types of churches still exist today amidst the slew of churches who may not operate in this way. And because we can read several books, blogs, and articles criticizing all the things the church gets wrong, I want to highlight the things that this type of church gets right.

One of the promises regarding receiving the Holy Spirit was that believers would receive power when the Holy Spirit has come upon them. This power would help Christ followers to be witnesses in Jerusalem, in all Judea and Samaria, and to the end of the earth. This power that the church was given empowers every Christian today to testify of the goodness of God, proclaiming the gospel of Jesus Christ, while helping us make disciples in all the earth.

As the early Christians walked this out, the church began to grow and "every day the Lord added to their number those who were being saved" (Acts 2:47). What strikes me in the book of Acts is, as the Holy Spirit empowers them as witnesses and the church grows, no one was left on the outskirts to simply figure this life out on their own. In Acts 2:44–45, we see that "all believers were together and held things in common. They sold their possessions and property and distributed the proceeds to all, as any had need."

We see this again in Acts 4:32–34. As the Holy Spirit empowers them to be witnesses, the church grows and the body of believers becomes one, loving each other in such a way that needs are met, people are healed, and the glory of Christ is shown. Although they are diligently walking out the call to be exiles collectively, living in this world yet not of it, there are no exiles among them. To be aware of one's needs and to move within your means to meet those needs takes intentionality within their communication and fellowship. In this type of church, those struggling with the reality of unanswered prayer, grief, and suffering can be encouraged in their faith through the kindness of the Lord shown through others.

As I write this, I think of the kindness of the Lord as shown from a church in Maryland toward my brother and sister-in-law. My youngest niece has a disability, and as my brother and sister-in-law began to visit the church, the leadership intentionally sought out ways to get to know our family. Upon learning about their child's needs, the leadership made sure those who may care for her in the children's church were trained to be able to serve our family well. They even purchased an additional walker, just for her to use when she is in church. When my niece has needed to visit the ER, people from the church take care of her sister. The church body has even graciously offered to assist with hospital bills if needed.

I am reminded of the kindness of the Lord shown from our church toward my family when my mom was diagnosed with sepsis and hospitalized. Because she has metastatic breast cancer, this condition was especially dangerous, and we are truly grateful the Lord brought her through. I remember our pastor's wife showing up at our house with a homecooked meal. At the time, my daughter Justice was two months old, and I was in the trenches of postpartum. The homecooked meals, the phone calls, and the prayer during that season was something I will never forget.

Perhaps you have your own stories of how your church body cared for you during a season of exile. And how you've been part of caring for others in an exile season.

A Needed Sidenote

Unfortunately, it doesn't always happen that way. Not everyone has had a positive experience from their church during difficult times. I've been in churches that haven't always made the right decisions, and they haven't always shown up for us and other members of their congregation as they ought. And maybe you have too.

Church hurt and spiritual abuse are real. My husband and I have lived through both, walking through deep disappointment from a church experience. There was a season we needed to step away to receive healing and to find a place that exhibits the characteristics shared in the beginning of this section. As we healed, we always knew we would return because by the grace of God, we still love the church deeply. We understand that there are flawed, sinful people who sit in our pews. And yet if all of our sin was on display to the world, we would all fall short. We too are flawed. Through it all, Christ's bride, the church, is still called to be a place for healing among healthy, compassionate community.

If you've experienced church hurt, I encourage you to not give up on the body of Christ but push through. As imperfect people, we will always find things that can improve in every congregation. Allow the Lord to lead you to your people, to a safe community where you can both serve and receive.

What Seasons of Exile Teach Us About God

When God feels the farthest away, He remains the most near. This is the omnipresence of God. This means that God, the Creator of space, is present everywhere. Even when we feel displaced and shifted into seasons of the unknown, God is there with us. David articulates this beautifully in Psalm 139:7–10:

> *Where can I go to escape your Spirit?*
> *Where can I flee from your presence?*
> *If I go up to heaven, you are there;*
> *if I make my bed in Sheol, you are there.*
> *If I fly on the wings of the dawn*
> *and settle down on the western horizon,*

> *even there your hand will lead me;*
> *your right hand will hold on to me.*

There is no place we can flee from the Lord's presence, and because God is sovereign, we can trust that He is leading us through the suffering this world so often brings.

We can also take comfort that we serve a God who is familiar with the feelings of abandonment as we walk through difficult times in our lives. As the sins of the world were placed on Jesus, experiencing horrific abuse on the cross, He cried out in the ninth hour, "'*Elí, Elí, lemá sabachtháni?*' that is, 'My God, my God, why have you forsaken me?'" (Matt. 27:46). Jesus Christ as the Son of God was divine, and He knew that His Father was with Him. Yet in that moment we also see Christ's humanity.

This moment of despair reminds us that we serve a High Priest who can empathize with our weaknesses (Heb. 4:15). And as the psalmist David so eloquently pens, "You yourself have recorded my wanderings. Put my tears in your bottle. Are they not in your book?" (Ps. 56:8). God doesn't just see what we are walking through. Our Lord knows every detail and is with us in it, producing endurance, character, and hope. And this kind of hope always wins, never fails, and won't disappoint (Rom. 5:4–5). It is this hope in the glory of Christ that is to come that shifts us to a place of joy.

> ∷ **TAKE A MOMENT**
> When you truly grasp the truth that God is always near, even when He feels far, how does this impact the season you are in today?

What Seasons of Exile Teach Us About Ourselves

Seasons of suffering often teach us more about ourselves than we expect. Through my last miscarriage I learned that, although I had been in Christ since 2005, I was broken and discontent. I had been so focused on conceiving that my spiritual disciplines began to dwindle. Sure, I prayed sporadically and I may have even read some Scripture, but there is truly a difference in how we engage with prayer and interact with the Scriptures when our heart is not there.

At the time, I was doing these things as a routine and not out of devotion. For this moment in my life, as a Christian, I had made conceiving a child an idol. Just as the Israelites trusted idols to fill their voids instead of allowing the one true and living God to fill that place, I too had found my idol. So when that idol was torn down and was not fulfilled, it devastated me.

I was turning forty, and I felt like my opportunities for having a family were dwindling. There were some difficult days as depression about my current state began to cloud my thoughts. I allowed these thoughts to consume me and the behaviors that followed were damaging to myself and my family. Months after the miscarriage, we reconnected to a healthy church community, and I reengaged in therapy. Pregnancy loss can be mentally and physically traumatic. We aren't meant to walk in the disappointment and sometimes trauma of unanswered prayers alone. Through God's abundant mercy, I was able to repent, heal in community, and allow God to restore my brokenness.

Getting Off the Island

When we are disappointed with people, we may take breaks from being with others or even sever relationships. However, when this type of behavior happens in our relationship with the

Lord, it is far more dangerous than we can imagine. Our disappointment must draw us closer. Our faith in who God is, His plans for us, and what is possible through Him must be like the parable of the persistent widow Jesus told in Luke 18:1–8.

> *Now he told them a parable on the need for them to pray always and not give up. "There was a judge in a certain town who didn't fear God or respect people. And a widow in that town kept coming to him, saying, 'Give me justice against my adversary.'*
>
> *"For a while he was unwilling, but later he said to himself, 'Even though I don't fear God or respect people, yet because this widow keeps pestering me, I will give her justice, so that she doesn't wear me out by her persistent coming.'"*
>
> *Then the Lord said, "Listen to what the unjust judge says. Will not God grant justice to his elect who cry out to him day and night? Will he delay helping them? I tell you that he will swiftly grant them justice. Nevertheless, when the Son of Man comes, will he find faith on earth?"*

This woman sought justice against her adversary from a judge who didn't fear God or respect people. She didn't care about her reputation or how her persistence made her look. "The key to the widow's persistence was her legal right to justice," Tony Evans clarifies.[3] What Jesus was explaining was that, if this judge who didn't care about God or people would help the widow because of her "legal right to justice," how much more will the God who loves and created us answer the prayers of those who belong to Him? These moments of displacement in our lives while we are waiting on answers from the Lord show us where our faith truly lies. "When the Son of Man comes," asks Jesus, "will he find faith on earth?"

Tony Evans adds, "Here is our willingness to persevere by faith in prayer based on God's Word. Believers, then, have a legal right to answered prayer."[4] While the answers to our prayers may not always happen on our timeline, or be answered in the way we expect, we can trust and have faith that He will indeed answer.

Every Christian will experience life cycles that mirror valleys, wilderness, and promised lands until we reach glory.

One of the things we can be sure of is that this feeling you may be experiencing today, the feeling of being displaced or exiled, perhaps on your personal island, won't last always. It can be a vulnerable yet beautiful place where you press into God's presence for the journey ahead. I wish I could give you a time stamp on when this season ends. It's different for all of us who land here throughout various times of our lives. Every Christian will experience life cycles that mirror valleys, wilderness, and promised lands until we reach glory. It's up to us to aggressively cling to Christ through them all.

↕ TAKE A MOMENT

Have you found yourself clinging to the potential gift of the answered prayer over the Giver? It's easy to unintentionally make an idol out of something we really want the Lord to do for us. When we've made this thing an idol, one of two things can happen: 1) When we receive the answer to our prayer, and it's what we've been desiring all along, we can still make an idol out of it; 2) We make an idol out of the thing we are desiring, and when it does not happen or the prayer is answered differently than we wanted, the result has the potential to shatter us. If you have found yourself in this space, take this moment to repent and ask the Lord for His forgiveness and guidance. Use this time to pray and ask the Lord to help you place Him in His rightful place in your heart.

4

Traverse

"For the LORD your God has blessed you in all the work of your hands. He has watched over your journey through this immense wilderness. The LORD your God has been with you these past forty years, and you have lacked nothing."

DEUTERONOMY 2:7

THE SPACE AND TIME BETWEEN prayer and an answer will vary in our lifetime. There are times where just as quickly as we have said the word "Amen," we see God move in a particular area. Then are those times when we find ourselves at the feet of Jesus and in our prayer closets lifting up our hearts' cry for years on end.

In-Between Silence

God often uses this space and time to grow us or to develop our faith. It's the space in between times of praying, seeking, and fasting that often is shrouded in silence as we seek answers.

This is the space between the disciples being in the middle of a great storm on the sea and when Jesus wakes up from His slumber to rebuke the winds.

It's the space between our receiving a grim prognosis to the answered prayers of the elders who anointed you and prayed for healing.

It's a moment of refinement. It's the intense heat and pressure rocks endure when becoming diamonds. It's where the trying of our faith produces patience. It is these moments in time that every believer must traverse as we cling to the hope that God is with us. This is also a place where temptation and vulnerability may often lurk to get our eyes off the joy that's set before us.

This is before the answered prayer and perhaps that collective sigh of relief that you made it to the other side. This is the wilderness. Let's hold on to that thought.

Traverse from Death to Life

I will always remember the day I repented of my sin and decided to trust Christ with my life.

In June 2004, at my mother's request, I attended a church overnight lock-in that the women's ministry was sponsoring. I asked my best friend to attend the event with me because I was twenty-four and far from the Lord, and I just didn't want to be around groups of church women alone without a close friend to hang out with. I needed my best friend for support so we could stick together and laugh at all of their churchy shenanigans.

To my surprise, she began engaging with the other women and enjoying herself. She simply could not help her outgoing personality. I admired that, but instead of joining in, I kept to myself, just waiting for the morning to come and the whole thing to be over. During one part of the event, the church's drama team performed a skit. I don't remember the details, but I do remember people in the audience crying. It was a powerful drama that communicated the gospel in a simple way that made me aware of my sin and need for Jesus.

I already knew parts of the gospel and had heard variations of it throughout my childhood in church. I grew up in northwest Washington, DC, with my parents, brother, grandfather, and eventually my aunt, uncle, and her four children. My aunt was the first churchgoing woman I ever encountered. She went to church every Sunday and brought her four small children along. And if there was a Sunday she needed to miss going, she would have church right in the living room and I would join them. We would read Scripture, she would teach us worship songs, and we would learn a Bible story right in the living room.

I began to join my aunt and her children at Abundant Life Faith Bible Church on some Sundays. I truly enjoyed children's church. Reading the stories in Scripture intrigued me and at times frightened me. Because my aunt talked a lot about what's often called the end times, I would have dreams of a time where Jesus would crack open the sky, trumpets would sound, and people would start disappearing. In some circles this is called the "rapture." In my dream, I would be left behind and begin praying and begging Jesus to take me too. Then I would wake up and run downstairs to see if my family was still there.

And so, as a child I became intrigued by the book of Revelation and its imagery, attempting to understand what it all meant. In children's church I was always raising my hand, engaging and answering the questions about the stories we read. The teacher saw my zeal and gave me my first non-children's Bible. It was a pocket-sized New Testament and in it she wrote that I would be a great woman of God one day. I didn't exactly know what all of that meant, but I was pleased she had given me the Bible.

At fourteen, my Sundays attending church abruptly came to an end as my parents decided to move. We'd been in a crowded home with a dozen people and now moved into our own apartment in southeast DC. It was during my teen years, away from the Spirit-filled, churchgoing covering of my aunt, that I began to explore all that I thought the world had to offer.

During this period between fourteen and twenty-four I often engaged in activities that brought me close to death. By the time I was at that church lock-in, I had lived a wild and dangerous lifestyle. I was broken and I knew it, but I didn't know a way out. My family wondered how I, a quiet and reserved bookworm who was always at the top of her class, had gotten to this place.

There was a prayer during the lock-in and an invitation to receive Jesus into our hearts and to allow the Holy Spirit to change our lives. I had heard this invitation before. I even responded to a few altar calls. But something about this time felt different. As everyone's head was bowed and eyes closed, I looked around to see the hands that went up in response to the invitation. I watched next to me as my best friend had her hand up. I thought, *If she has her hand up, Lord knows I need my hand up.* And so, I followed her lead. I knew I desperately needed my life to change.

Shortly after the prayer, we were led to a room in the back of the church to learn more about following Jesus and the commitment we had made to the Lord. We were able to ask questions and pray with somebody one-on-one. I had been to church in the past, I enjoyed the Bible stories, but on that day in June 2004, something shifted. When I returned home to a relationship I had no business being in, it felt wrong for the first time. I was no longer comfortable in the sin I was in and began truly trying to understand who I was and who God was.

Early Days with the Lord

I remember those first days and weeks in Christ. It felt like a veil had been lifted, and I could see the light at the end of the tunnel. I felt like I was running through meadows of green grass and flowers with *The Sound of Music* playing in the background. I began to pray for the first time, and it seemed like every time I would pray, the Lord would answer my prayer shortly thereafter. I would boast in the Lord regularly! I knew He was real! He allowed me to get a new job making more money. Things were looking up for me and I knew it was all the Lord.

When my friends at the time invited me to go to the gay pride festivities in Atlanta for Labor Day weekend, I saw it as an opportunity to let my hair down and celebrate. I didn't have any Christian friends, and although the Lord had changed my heart, at the time I was still hanging around with and influenced by the same people. Sanctification, or becoming holy, is indeed a process, and I was at the very beginning.

I remember getting a call from my best friend checking on me to see if I had landed at the airport. I told her yes and that I would call her when I get home. Unfortunately, I would never get to make that call.

An Unwelcome Development

It was September 5, 2004. My best friend, the one who had rededicated her life to the Lord three months before—the one who was planning her daughter's one-year-old birthday party, the beautiful, outgoing, intelligent woman who just graduated from university—was shot and soon declared brain dead.

When I got the phone call, I immediately called my mom and asked her to pray. She met me at the hospital as I ran down the hall in between the crowds of people to see my friend. I was determined that the God we had just prayed to three months ago to come into our hearts and save us was going to save her from the damage of the gunshot.

I touched my best friend's hand, which was still warm, as my own hot tears streamed down my face. My mom and I began to plead with the Lord for a miracle. We prayed for Him to do what the doctors were now saying was impossible. We prayed for her to wake up from her coma because she had an eleven-month-old daughter who needed her. Her mother, father, fiancé, and little sister needed her. I needed her. On September 6, 2004, the life support was removed and she went to be in the presence of the Lord.

Questions

I had questions.

I did not understand why this had happened and why God didn't heal her.

I read that He raised Lazarus from the dead, opened blind eyes, and more. I knew that He could heal my friend, but this prayer wasn't answered, and I didn't understand why.

Where I once felt like my faith in Christ had me running through meadows of flowers like in *The Sound of Music*, it now felt like I was trudging through the wilderness.

It was the first time in my new Christian walk where I would have to learn what it looked like to trust God when I didn't understand what was happening or why. Have you been to a place like that?

In their well-meaning attempts to comfort, people told us all kinds of things. "God wanted a new flower for

> *I will never be able to explain why terrible things happen. But I can share about the goodness of God.*

His garden and so He picked her." Well, why wouldn't He just create a new flower instead of allowing a new mom and a new convert to die in such a horrible way?

"Well, God is allowing this to make you stronger." Well, Lord, why didn't You just give me strength to weight train instead of trying to make me strong in this way? Yeah, that didn't feel right either.

Some moments in life we end up in the hardest situations and we don't have an answer. And that's okay. It really is. It takes a while to get to that place of accepting that we will never understand everything about this world and yet continuing to live in the goodness of God. I will never be able to explain to my goddaughter why this happened to her mother. But I can share with her about the goodness of God. And how when we don't understand, we simply cling to what we know. We know that He is good. He walked with her family through this horrible tragedy. Many people grew in their relationship and dependence on the Lord during this challenging time. This death was not in vain. God was and continues to be glorified over twenty years later in the lives that she touched.

The Lord Brings Us to the Wilderness

During my early days of walking with the Lord I wondered why our lives couldn't just be filled with good cheer and good times. I guess I wanted Christianity to look more like Christmas with Jesus being our Santa Claus bringing us every present we asked for if we were "good" people on our best behavior. And so, I began to check things off my list I needed to fix. I needed to be celibate, I had to find a way to stop cursing, I threw away my CDs, replaced my hip hop with all gospel genres (this was in the early 2000s before streaming), and finally I had to stop drinking alcohol and smoking marijuana.

It was time to be on my best behavior for Jesus because I wanted Him to bless me. I was operating on a works-based salvation that didn't exist because I had been taught that was the way I could make whatever I desired happen. However, I could not understand why God would allow His children, who have committed their lives to Christ, to experience a wilderness. Yes, I knew that God is good. But why would a good God bring us to the wilderness when He has all the power to bring us right into whatever promised land we are praying for?

It's an honest question most Christians have asked at some point.

Knowing Jesus

To answer this question is to understand who Jesus is, His life, ministry, and purpose for all humankind. Jesus humbled Himself by becoming a servant and coming to earth as a man.

Before beginning His ministry, He spent time fasting and praying in the wilderness for forty days and forty nights. He was tempted by Satan and passed every test. As we've said, He can "sympathize with our weaknesses" because He was tempted just as we are, "but without sin" (Heb. 4:15).

The Son of God experienced life on earth as we do, the joys and sorrows. He spent time teaching, attending meals with friends, traveling. He grieved the death of a beloved friend named Lazarus. He suffered betrayal by His disciple Judas, and His good friend Peter even denied that he knew Him.

He experienced extreme pain through beatings, piercing of the flesh, and being hung on a cross. Jesus, who exists outside of time and eternity, allowed Himself to live on earth with a human body and experience the death that we deserved.

Christ was without sin, and because He is God in the flesh, He could have chosen to end it all right there. He could have become the Marvel Movie Jesus and strike everyone dead, leaving us to suffer for all eternity with no atonement for our sins.

Nonetheless, the unconditional love of Christ motivated Him to empty Himself, taking on the form of a servant, and taking on the likeness of humanity (Phil. 2:7). I believe a part of knowing who Jesus is requires us to be able relate to Him as He relates to us and all that we experience in this fallen world.

Christ with Us

To truly know and understand this type of love is to be able to experience the grace, love, and peace of Christ in the midst of our own suffering. While experiencing his own suffering in prison, the apostle Paul says in Philippians 3:10–11: "My goal is to know him and the power of his resurrection and the fellowship of his sufferings, being conformed to his death, assuming that I will somehow reach the resurrection from among the dead."

To know Christ, the power of His resurrection, and the fellowship of His sufferings is to be closely associated with the things Jesus experienced. Our suffering is an invitation to know Christ intimately. Clinging to Christ as our lifeline as we traverse the wilderness gives us the strength to keep moving. This is why, when we are traversing the wilderness, clinging to Christ through prayer is necessary. He is our present help because He understands and sympathizes.

Jesus has experienced these moments of heartache and disappointment and still was without sin. So as we walk through what feels like the wilderness in our lives, Jesus calls us to greater intimacy with Him. Where we are weak, He is our strength, giving us an invitation to "approach the throne of grace with boldness, so that we may receive mercy and find grace to help us in time of need" (Heb. 4:16).

> :: **TAKE A MOMENT**
>
> Have you approached the throne of grace with boldness? What is that secret prayer of your heart that you have not spoken? Take this time to journal and pray that prayer. This is your moment to receive mercy and grace. The Lord is with you. He hears you. And wants to go with you through the wilderness.

This is a prayer that Christ honors from those who are His followers. We have this access to our Father in heaven to boldly ask God to act. His eyes are on the righteous and His ears are open to our cries for help (Ps. 34:15). What would happen if we allowed the wilderness to draw us to intense prayer and communication with the Father?

The Place of Preparation

Throughout Scripture, wherever you see a wilderness experience, you will see a sovereign God leading His people to these desolate places. Let's examine these experiences:

- You might be familiar with the story of Joseph in the Bible; you can read the first part of it in Genesis 37. Briefly, Joseph's brothers were jealous of him and threw him into a pit. His brother Reuben intended to pull him out later. He said to his brothers, "'Don't shed blood. Throw him into this pit in the wilderness but don't lay a hand on him'—intending to rescue him from them and return him to his father" (Gen. 37:22).

Before Reuben had a chance to return, the other brothers had sold Joseph into slavery.

- The Lord led Moses and all of Israel into a journey in the wilderness. They would be there until they reached Canaan, a land flowing with milk and honey. Initially this journey should have taken eleven days. However, due to the unbelief, rebellion, and idol worship of God's people, their journey in the wilderness lasted forty years. "Your children will be shepherds in the wilderness for forty years and bear the penalty for your acts of unfaithfulness until all your corpses lie scattered in the wilderness. You will bear the consequences of your iniquities forty years based on the number of the forty days that you scouted the land, a year for each day" (Num. 14:33–34).

These were people who experienced the manifest presence of God, who saw His glory, along with signs and wonders. However, they still chose to walk in disobedience. In their case, the wilderness was a consequence of their sin. Wilderness is not always a consequence of our sin, but we can use the Israelites' experiences as an example to trust in the Lord as we traverse difficult times. We are to set our eyes on Him as He guides us, while resisting the temptation to erect idols in our own lives as distractions or coping mechanisms.

- John the Baptist preached in the wilderness of Judea for people to "prepare the way for the Lord; make his paths straight!" (Matt. 3:3). As he urged people to repent and be baptized, Jesus also came to be baptized. Following His baptism, Jesus was led into the wilderness by the Holy Spirit to be tempted by the devil. The wilderness was a time of prayer and preparation that would strengthen our Lord for His time of ministry, which was roughly three years before His crucifixion and resurrection. "Then Jesus was led up by the Spirit into the wilderness to be tempted by the devil" (Matt. 4:1).

In each of these cases the wilderness was a temporary place of preparation. It was a time where the people of God could purpose themselves to hear from God and, like Joseph, they could experience God's hand in unexpected yet intentional ways.

> **TAKE A MOMENT**
> What is the Lord doing with you in this season? How have you seen His hand guiding and developing you? Take time to meditate on how you've seen Him as you traverse this time in your life.

"God, Where Are You?"

In some of the hardest wilderness moments of our lives, this question may come to mind: "God, where are You?" As we wait for the Lord to show up a certain way, or even just coming to the realization that He is with us while we wait, we must resist the temptation to be our own God. When we try to take matters into our own hands outside of what the Lord is actually leading us to do, we can often cause more harm than good. We see this as the Israelites impatiently wait for Moses to return from Mount Sinai with the Ten Commandments.

> *When the people saw that Moses delayed in coming down from the mountain, they gathered around Aaron and said to him, "Come, make gods for us who will go before us because*

this Moses, the man who brought us up from the land of Egypt—we don't know what has happened to him!" (EX. 32:1)

In my own life as I've traversed various wildernesses, I face temptation to lean into temporary fixes to numb the current reality. I have found myself being hit with horrible news and instead of running to the throne of grace, I've run to the throne of the phone.

Let us examine the idols we may erect as we wait and go through the wilderness. Have you ever been in a hard season and have found yourself mindlessly scrolling through social media or the internet for answers? Even now, as my mother received news that the cancer in her body was no longer responding to the medicine she was prescribed, I had to physically remove myself from my computer because I began researching endlessly for answers. This is not to say that researching is wrong. It's wise to seek counsel and to research for the answers you may need.

Yet, as I researched, I realized that anxiety began to creep into my body as I felt fear take over my mind. When I stepped away from the computer and began to quiet my mind through prayer, the anxiety began to cease.

> *Sometimes instead of running to the throne of grace, I've run to the throne of the phone.*

He Is Near

Casting our cares on the One who ultimately cares for us and who has the power to shift whatever we are going through is where I needed to be. And although we may be in the middle of waiting for specific answers to prayers from the Lord, our communion with the Holy Spirit provides the immediate answer to what we need the most.

God has many titles and names in the Bible. He is the Great I Am. Interestingly, the Hebrew word for "I am" is where the name Yahweh is derived. He is also "Immanuel," which means "God is with us." He is near. He is here. Christ is our answer, our redemption, and Savior, and we have the means to communicate with Him in the wilderness as He guides us through.

From the beginning of time, Yahweh has desired to commune with His creation. Throughout the Old Testament we see God responding to the cries and prayers of His people through various means. As God called Moses to lead the Israelites out of captivity, He showed up as fire within a burning bush and communicated audibly to Moses. And as Moses led the Israelites out of Egypt, the events we call the Exodus, "the LORD went ahead of them in a pillar of a cloud to lead them on their way during the day and in a pillar of fire to give them light at night, so that they could travel day or night" (Ex. 13:21).

In the New Testament, we see the Living Word, God in the flesh, Jesus Christ who comes from heaven to earth to lead and guide in His ministry with the disciples. Through His time of ministry, as He prepares to take on the sins of the world, we learn how Jesus engages and communicates with others. Toward the end of His time on earth, He promises another Counselor who would be with us forever (John 14:16). This Counselor is the Holy Spirit, who dwells with all believers.

Today, we do not need to experience the manifest presence of God through pillars of fire or Him walking with us in the flesh. But we have a greater gift: the gift of the Holy Spirit to lead and guide us into all truth, to comfort, and to always dwell with each believer. What a gift! We are never without Him.

The Holy Spirit isn't a mere presence, force, or a feeling. The Holy Spirit is the third person of the Trinity. When we understand that the Holy Spirit is a person as are the Father and Son, our perspective is expanded. He walks with us, lives on the inside of us, and He's consistently there to comfort, counsel, teach, and lead. For the believer, "God with us" is not just a cool phrase. He first has drawn us to surrender and then is with us from the day we begin to trust Christ.

If you've ever had the thought, *Why can't I hear Him?* you are not alone. There are periods of time as we traverse where things do seem quiet. It's in those times I encourage you to lean into the quiet and practice solitude.

Solitude is a spiritual discipline that we must not fail to neglect in our practices. It requires us to pull away to pray and hear from the Lord. Noises and distractions in our world can prevent us from leaning into hearing from the Holy Spirit. This is why it's critical to traverse with intention as we purpose ourselves to hear from the Lord.

He Is in the Solitude

During Jesus' ministry, He often went to desolate places within the mountains alone to pray. He understood the power of community as He did life daily with the disciples. And He also understood the importance of solitude, retreating often to the mountaintop to pray after times of ministry. If Jesus did this, how much more do we need to intentionally take time to pray and hear from the Holy Spirit? The beautiful thing about the Lord is that He also gave us sixty-six books of Holy Spirit–inspired words to meditate on. God spoke on every page of Scripture, and if we need a word from Him, we always have His words at hand.

The deception that comes in the wilderness is the feeling of being all alone. Yes, there may be a season where we have to endure and walk through some things, but if you are in Christ, you are never truly alone. "Be satisfied with what you have, for he himself has said, I will never leave you or abandon you" (Heb. 13:5). The God who was with Joseph and Moses and the Israelites and countless multitudes of others through their entire wilderness journeys is the same God who is with you today.

With all that we walk through on earth, whether miscarriages, marital challenges, the deep longing for a spouse, job loss, feeling stuck in our careers, caregiving for an elderly parent, finances, challenges with mental illness, and so much more—you can simply fill in the blank here. We don't walk through these things without the person of the Holy Spirit accompanying us. When we are in the thick of it (whatever your *it* is), it may feel like you are the only person in the world going through it. But not only is the Lord with you in it, there are other saints all over the globe who are experiencing similar things. Trials are not always a result of something we did. Sometimes this is just the part of our journey that simply just *is*. And even so, while there may be many reasons we are brought to this moment, what we can be sure of is that God is good through it all.

∷ TAKE A MOMENT

Pause here and look at your schedule. Plan a time of solitude with the Lord. Try not to play music or answer the phone during this time. You want to be fully present with the Holy Spirit. Pray and ask Him to lead and guide your time together. Try to do this for at least thirty minutes or longer. Journal the things you may receive in prayer.

The Promised Land

Every generation has its promised land. *Webster's Dictionary* defines promised land as "something and especially a place or condition believed to promise final satisfaction or a realization of hopes."[1] For the Israelites, their promised land was the land of Canaan flowing with milk and honey. For African Americans experiencing chattel slavery, their promised land was the states up north or even cities overseas where physical freedom was available.

Dr. Martin Luther King spoke of a "promised land" in his speech "I See the Promised Land" given on April 3, 1968, in Memphis, Tennessee.[2] This promised land pertained to freedom from racial and economic inequality. Marcus Garvey, activist and founder of the Universal Negro Improvement Association (UNIA), created a "Back to Africa" movement.[3] This movement encouraged Black Americans to focus inward, looking within ourselves and to Africa for our own promised land. For some today, getting to the promised land means achieving the American Dream, whatever that might mean to different people.

I believe we all desire to reach a "promised land," a place of rest that we long to experience in this lifetime. As the psalmist declares in Psalm 27:13, "I am certain that I will see the Lord's goodness in the land of the living." Our promised land can be a time where we have walked out of the valley and the wilderness seasons of life and into places where we can exhale.

Maybe it's the long-awaited moment when you can embrace the daughter who has been far from the Lord and has made the decision to come home.

Maybe you find yourself ringing the bell of completion because the Lord has brought you through cancer treatments.

Maybe you have gotten a grip on your finances.

Whatever that moment is for you, we all desire to experience the joy of reaching the *promised land*. This is the internal satisfaction that God has brought us through to the other side.

Yet like the Israelites, we will often experience several seasons traversing various wildernesses throughout our lives. We are either in a trial, on our way to experiencing a trial, or we are getting out of a trial. Some wildernesses feel harder and longer and more treacherous than others. There are also times where we find ourselves going around the same mountainous problem and can't seem to find our way out.

But how do we keep moving through them all? What do we do with our unanswered prayers or when the wilderness feels like it will never end?

Only God knows when your wilderness will end—but there will be an end. At some point in our journey we will have what I like to describe as a "promised land moment." Much like the Israelites who journeyed through the wilderness for forty years, at some point we may enter that promised land or that "answered prayer" time in our lives. This promised land moment comes with relief and immense gratitude. It also comes with its own unique set of challenges. For the Israelites who prepared to enter the land of Canaan flowing with milk and honey, they came up against something they did not expect:

> *[The scouts] reported to Moses, "We went into the land where you sent us. Indeed it is flowing with milk and honey, and here is some of its fruit. However, the people living in the land are strong, and the cities are large and fortified . . . and all the people we saw in it are men of great size."* (NUM. 13:27–28, 32)

Crossing over into the land of Canaan would not be without opposition. The people Moses and Aaron were leading began to doubt God's promises after being sent to spy out land and noticing the strength of those whose land they were to take possession of. Even though the promised land was in front of them, they continued to fall into the temptation of doubting God. Yes, the prayer was answered, but there were also new challenges ahead of them that would test and try their faith.

The person who received a long-awaited promotion on the job with a sizable salary increase may also be challenged with the new staff they have to manage. There may be a higher level of administrative work that needs to be completed. They may miss out on time with their children due to their commitments at work and struggle with rhythms of rest.

The woman who finally gets pregnant and has the baby they have prayed for years to have may now wrestle with postpartum depression, feeling left out, postpartum hair loss, and exorbitant daycare/nanny costs.

The single who gets married after years of being on her own may now wrestle with sharing a home with her husband who isn't as neat as she expected. If she's maintained a celibate lifestyle for many years, she may also have challenges with adapting to a consistent sexual routine with her husband.

All in all, our promised land moments are also designed to push us to cling to Christ. We must develop a lifestyle of clinging to Christ in the wilderness and on the mountaintop, in the valley and on the plain. We continue to cling to Christ because our ultimate hope is in Him, and Christ is able to bring us through every season of life.

Ultimately, there is a promised land for believers that will not simply be a moment in time that will give way to a new season of challenges. This is the promised land in the "new Jerusalem," a holy city for God's people described in Revelation 21:1–4:

> *Then I saw a new heaven and a new earth, for the first heaven and the first earth had passed away, and the sea was no more. I also saw the holy city, the new Jerusalem, coming down out of heaven from God, prepared like a bride adorned for her husband.*
>
> *Then I heard a loud voice from the throne. Look, God's dwelling is with humanity, and he will live with them. They will be his peoples, and God himself will be with them and will be their God. He will wipe away every tear from their eyes. Death will be no more; grief, crying, and pain will be no more, because the previous things have passed away.*

There is an expiration date to all of our pain and suffering. This may not sound hopeful while you are in the thick of whatever it is you are traversing. But go with me for a minute. Go back and reread these verses above. Then close your eyes and let's imagine this place together. This imagination isn't something that we are making up in our heads. God's Word is true, and there will be a time when every tear is wiped from our eyes—death, grief, crying, and pain will be no more.

And even more exciting than all of that, we will have an opportunity to experience God dwelling with humanity. For those who are in Christ, the end is simply a new beginning. That's something that often through tears I've had to remind myself even as I rejoice as I see God's goodness in my promised land moments. There is something far greater and more satisfying to look forward to.

May we live in light of that truth traversing with Christ here on earth until we traverse to Him in eternity.

5

Prodigal

So he got up and went to his father. But while the son was still a long way off, his father saw him and was filled with compassion.

LUKE 15:20

I'VE ALWAYS RELATED TO THE parable of the prodigal son in Luke 15. Jesus begins to tell this well-known story along with others to Pharisees and teachers of the law who were upset that He would eat with "sinful" people.

In this particular parable we meet a man with two sons. The younger son wanted his share of his father's estate before his father died. The father agreed to divide his assets between his sons, and the younger son gathered his share and quickly squandered his money by living recklessly. Desperate, he began to work for one of the citizens in that country who sent him to the fields to feed pigs. It got to a point where the young man was so hungry he longed to be fed with the slop the pigs were eating. At some point, he has an epiphany and remembers how his father's hired servants are fed. He decides to return home to repent before his father and ask if he could be a mere servant.

Prodigal Moments

Maybe we all have experienced this moment. Our moments of "Prodigal Past" are our pre-Christ moments. We were lost and then found by a compassionate God who saw us in our sin, relentlessly sought us, drew us to Himself, and redeemed us.

Then there are moments where we may experience a "Prodigal Present." These are times in our lives as believers when we may drift and need to reconnect to our Father. I believe this parable shows us who God is as a compassionate Father during times when we need to be fathered the most.

My favorite part in the parable is found in Luke 15:20: "So he got up and went to his father. But while the son was still a long way off, his father saw him and was filled with compassion." Two things stand out here. The first is seeing the son get up and go to his father while at a very low point in his life. He had squandered the assets that were given to him with "foolish living" (v. 13).

> *If you are in a place of regret, it's never too late to turn from sin and turn to Christ.*

We don't exactly know what that foolish living was, but simply imagine your own times of foolish living. I'm sure you can relate. When we are in dark places it is easy to remain there. Yet darkness will always produce more darkness. May we find ourselves like the son who was lost and push ourselves to the light. If we don't repent and run to the Father, we may find ourselves in places and situations we will regret. And even if you are already in this place of regret, it's never too late to turn from sin and turn to Christ. We must push past what we may feel, confessing our sin to a holy and just God who loves us and is waiting to restore.

We also notice in this passage that while the son is still far off, the father sees him, has compassion on him, and runs toward his son. The father in this parable didn't wait for his son to fix everything before he came to him. He met him right where he was in his mess. How beautiful is that? You may feel like you are in a place of no return. That perhaps this sin that you are wrestling with is too deep for you to be in fellowship with God. And I am here to tell you that there is nothing that the Lord hasn't seen. He already knew you would be in that place, and He is there waiting to love you back to life. Like the prodigal son, we must humble ourselves and confess our sins to our Father, allowing restoration to begin to take place.

How Did We Get Here?

There's always a moment when, like the lost son, we look up from our own pig slop and wonder, "How did I get here?" How would you answer that question? Could it be because you were angry at God because a prayer was not answered as you expected, and you started to take matters into your own hands and failed? Perhaps it was because you are disappointed and just simply tired of waiting. When we have found ourselves in "pig slop," it's usually because we have forgotten who God is in our lives. Just as the lost son had an epiphany where he realized, "I don't have to live this way; I have a father who takes care of his servants better than this," we have to remember that we have a good Father, and we can live in a way that honors Him through our disappointment.

No matter how long we've been following Christ, we'll have times when we are faced with the realization, "I know better than this. What am I doing?" As we come to grips with the answers, we must begin a process of acknowledgment, confession, and repentance before healing can take place. Acknowledgment is critical and something that cannot be glossed over. We must stare at the ugliness of our pride, envy, lust, gossip, deceit, or whatever sin you find yourself in. No matter how big or small we think it is, we must acknowledge that this is now an issue. If you belong to Christ, what you are experiencing is grievous to you because of the Holy Spirit who dwells within you. Whatever this thing is may keep you up at night praying as you wrestle. You aren't comfortable in this place, which is a positive catalyst for change. You acknowledge that this is a struggle, and it's time to wrestle through this and overcome with Christ.

Beware of Vulnerability

Grief, suffering, disappointment, and unresolved/unhealed pain can be gateways to our vulnerability to sin. When we are vulnerable, we are more open to being wounded in some way, and many of these wounds are actually self-inflicted. When that happens, we must be careful not to wound ourselves or allow the enemy to take advantage of our weakness.

Discontentment, depression, discouragement, comparison, impatience, unhealthy coping mechanisms, and even reckless behavior may often lurk in the shadows. I have learned that after my pregnancy losses I was most prone to the sins of comparison, covetousness, and envy. During tough seasons of marriage, I have found that I was susceptible to lust. Some who are single for longer periods of time than they desire may wrestle with comparison or the desire to engage in porn. And perhaps there was a time where you drowned your disappointment with overeating or overindulgence in other things. Wherever you find yourself, the Lord has a way of escape for you.

As Peter wrote to those living as exiles who were Christians dispersed to various Gentile nations,

> *Be sober-minded, be alert. Your adversary the devil is prowling around like a roaring lion, looking for anyone he can devour. Resist him, firm in the faith, knowing that the same kind of sufferings are being experienced by your fellow believers throughout the world.* (1 PETER 5:8–9)

In areas where we may be vulnerable, we must be attentive to resisting temptation and remaining firm in our faith. There are times where I've been on the vigilant side with resisting and fleeing the enemy and there have been times I've failed miserably. During those times, Christian community has been a healing balm. If you are in this space, there may be a temptation to retreat and isolate. No matter what, resist that temptation! We all need safe places where we can confess sin to trusted mature believers. "Confess your sins to one another and pray for one another, so that you may be healed. The prayer of a righteous person is very powerful in its effect" (James 5:16).

We must also purpose in our hearts to be that safe place for someone else. If you don't have that safe space where you can confess your sins and receive prayer from another sister or brother in Christ, begin to pray and ask the Lord to reveal that person to you. Pray for wisdom on how to cultivate those relationships and support one another in prayer.

> **∷ TAKE A MOMENT**
> Can someone confess an area of sin to you that they are wrestling with and it not become gossip? Can they find in you a person who will listen, pray, and point them to Scripture? Do you also have these kinds of people in your life?

Life will undoubtedly throw curveballs and gut punches. How these gut punches impact us will always show how deep or how shallow our roots are. It will show if we are standing on a firm foundation or simply coasting through life on shaky ground. It will reveal if we've been abiding in Christ or trusting in our own strength.

Lavish Son, Lavish Father

In learning this story and hearing it be preached many times, I've always viewed it from the standpoint of the lost son. And while that is accurate, the definition of prodigal reveals much more. A prodigal is "one who spends or gives lavishly and foolishly."[1] This son who lavishly spends and wastes his inheritance is able to return to his father who then bestows nothing but the best on his son.

> *But the father told his servants, "Quick! Bring out the best robe and put it on him; put a ring on his finger and sandals on his feet. Then bring the fattened calf and slaughter it, and let's celebrate with a feast!"* (LUKE 15:22–23)

The father's behavior in this parable is a reminder of the extravagance of our heavenly Father's love. It is a picture of the gospel to know that in our dark "pig slop" moments, we serve a God who loved us enough to send Jesus to pay the price for our sins. This is the greatest gift, but the Lord doesn't just stop there. Just as the father in this parable has his servants bring the best robe to place on his son, so it is with Christ and His lavish love covering a multitude of sins (1 Peter 4:8).

Can you think about a time where God's mercy and grace covered you? When the enemy desires to expose the dark places to our detriment, the Lord's desire is to cover us, giving us the opportunity to turn away from our sin and return to the Father's arms. In the parable, the father placed a signet ring on his son's hand and brought out the "best robe." Both the robe and the ring had great significance in this culture. "The best robe was a sign of position and the ring also, especially if, as many hold, a signet ring is [what is] meant (cf. Gen. 41:42; Est. 3:10; 8:2); such a ring conveyed authority."[2] These items identified his son as connected to this family line. It speaks to the beauty of Christ who gives us our identity. Once we are in Christ, our identity is not connected to or defined by what we've done, but who we serve and follow.

> *Once we are in Christ, our identity is not connected to or defined by what we've done, but who we serve and follow.*

The Good Shepherd

Who better knows the character of the Father than the Son, who is our Good Shepherd? In another parable in the gospel of Matthew, Jesus tells the story of the lost sheep.

> *"What do you think? If someone has a hundred sheep, and one of them goes astray, won't he leave the ninety-nine on the hillside and go and search for the stray? And if he finds it, truly I tell you, he rejoices over that sheep more than over the ninety-nine that did not go astray. In the same way, it is not the will of your Father in heaven that one of these little ones perish."* (MATT. 18:12–14)

How beautiful is our Father's love! He doesn't leave us in areas of unrighteousness to die in our sin. He consistently draws us, comes after us, and gives us opportunities to restore our relationship with Him.

Job held on to his integrity throughout all his horrible trials. Maybe you had a trial but, unlike Job, you were unable to hang on to your integrity. Maybe you know the verse about resisting the devil—"Resist the devil and he will flee from you" (James 4:7)—but when the situation came up, you failed to resist in some area of your life.

Don't ignore the nudging of the Good Shepherd to reconcile and get back in good standing. It may be the nudge of realizing you're using alcohol to cope, or you're using social media or television to drown out what you are feeling. We must listen to these nudges that the Good Shepherd gives. These areas of sin may seem harmless at the moment, but they often grow, and like anything else they can become habitual in our lives. Our Good Shepherd desires the best for us. Oftentimes these nudges—the still, small voice from the Holy Spirit, and sometimes the loud in-our-face voice from a friend, pastor, parent, or mentor who hears from the Lord—are exactly what we need to adhere to as we begin to turn things around.

There were times after some of the biggest heartbreaks of my life, such as the loss of my father and losing children through miscarriages, where I had to fight to restore my view of God. I grew up attending churches whose theology taught me that suffering was a result of not having enough faith; this false belief was in the undercurrent of my anger with God. This anger at the Father I loved resulted in my reading the Bible and praying less, when I should have been seeking the face of Christ more.

I learned a hard lesson in those seasons: You cannot pull yourself out of the pig slop! As Paul shared in 1 Corinthians, we need strength beyond our human ability that comes from the Good Shepherd.

> *Therefore, so that I would not exalt myself, a thorn in the flesh was given to me, a messenger of Satan to torment me so that I would not exalt myself. Concerning this, I pleaded with the Lord three times that it would leave me. But he said to me, "My grace is sufficient for you, for my power is perfected in weakness."* (2 COR. 12:7–9)

We don't know what Paul's specific thorn in his flesh was. He prayed to the Lord three times that it would leave him. Whatever this affliction was, Paul prayed about it and yet it was not taken from him. What we do know is that it tormented him, keeping him in a place of humility knowing that He needed the Lord's grace to power through. Instead of allowing this thorn to draw him away from Christ, he ran toward Him.

:: **TAKE A MOMENT**
Have you been receiving these nudges from the Holy Spirit to repent in a specific area of your life? Quiet your mind. Breathe in peace. Exhale the forgiveness of the Lord.

> Remember that Christ's strength is made perfect in your weakness. Take the time you need at this moment to pray, confessing your sin, knowing that Christ is faithful and just to cleanse you and forgive you of all unrighteousness (see 1 John 1:9).

Who Am I Now?

Now that you've repented and returned if needed, please remember these words: You are not the worst thing that you've done. As I shared earlier, your identity is not connected to who you were at your worst moments. Coming to terms with what we've done is important, but what's even more critical is that we learn to receive God's forgiveness.

The father in the prodigal son parable put things on his son (robe and ring) that signified his son's connection, authority, and identity in relation to him. Our heavenly Father clothes us with the blood of His Son, Jesus Christ, which signifies our connection, authority, and identity as sons and daughters of the Father.

Shame was introduced to our world through sin in the garden of Eden. From the beginning of time, shame was a way the enemy sought to push people away from God. When Adam and Eve ate the forbidden fruit from the tree of the knowledge of good and evil, they immediately were made aware of their sin, and shame entered their lives. We should experience godly sorrow over our sin, which draws us to the Lord for repentance as we recognize our need for Christ. However, shame often brings us into condemnation and hiding. Condemnation over sin can bring us to places of hopelessness where people tend to draw away from the only One who has the power to save.

In Genesis 3, we see Adam and Eve hiding under fig leaves in the garden as if they could hide from Yahweh (the Great I Am). "Then the man and his wife heard the sound of the LORD God walking in the garden at the time of the evening breeze, and they hid from the LORD God among the trees of the garden" (Gen. 3:8). Shame will keep us in bondage to sin if we allow it. It then becomes difficult to move forward and receive God's forgiveness to us through our repentance. As we face these things head on, acknowledging our struggles, confessing our sin to a trusted community, and receiving the forgiveness of the Lord, restoration can begin to take place.

Resorative Correction

As a child, one of the things my father always cautioned me about was to never play in the street. I could play outside in our neighborhood and in the front yard. But I should never play in the street due to the potential danger of being hit by a car.

On one summer day, I was playing tag with a girl in our neighborhood. I found the perfect hiding place: behind the bumper of a large blue Cadillac. In the midst of the game, I forgot about my father's instructions. I was solely focused on the fun I was having. The thought of danger was far from my mind. As I was hiding behind the car, somehow my father found me.

This was not the person I wanted to find me, but as he pulled me out of the street, I quickly remembered that I was not supposed to be there and began to cry. My father took me into his arms, into our house, and lovingly disciplined me. He wanted to know why I had disobeyed him. The truth was, I got lost in my own desire to play. I didn't want to be restricted.

Nonetheless, I learned a valuable lesson that day. If I was ever walking into danger as a result of my own disobedience, my father would do his best to discipline me in a way that was clear and taught me a lesson, but without shame. At times, this was effective and other times not so much. Funny how we can often learn so much about God the Father through our relationships with our own fathers whether they are good or whether they have challenges. Much like my father, our heavenly Father is always there watching, protecting, guiding, and leading us back to Him. And when we need it, He lovingly disciplines us:

> *My son, do not regard lightly the discipline of the Lord,*
> *nor be weary when reproved by him.*
> *For the Lord disciplines the one he loves,*
> *and chastises every son whom he receives.* (HEB. 12:5–6 ESV[3])

The Greek word translated "discipline" in this passage means to instruct, train, teach, or correct. With Christ's love and compassion comes correction. At times this is a gentle nudge from the Holy Spirit, and other times it feels like a smack upside our head or someone shaking our shoulders telling us to "get it together." However the discipline comes, it is for our benefit so that we can share in His holiness (Heb. 12:10). This is a part of our sanctification process as we are daily being formed into the image of Christ. Correction often shows up as pruning. This pruning reveals areas where we have missed the mark and cuts various things out of our lives so that we can bear more of the fruit of the Holy Spirit: "But the fruit of the Spirit is love, joy, peace, patience, kindness, goodness, faithfulness, gentleness, and self-control" (Gal. 5:22–23).

Correction from Fellow Christians

We've all seen it happen. Someone apparently falls from grace in an area and fellow Christians begin to flood their timelines, direct messages, and social media posts with comments of disappointment. Christian magazines and blogs begin to report on the matter if the person is of some notable status. And the firestorm of opinions begins on that individual and whatever it is they are dealing with.

I must admit, I've been one of those people, self-righteously adding my comment to a situation even though I have no idea what's really happening behind the scenes. And in many cases, we feel like our statements are warranted. But as I've experienced life, and my own convictions around this have come to the surface, I've started to wonder if this is the way Christ wants us to handle these occurrences.

As we reflect on the parable of the lost son, we cannot forget there was another son who was impacted by these events. This son was bothered watching the father lavish his love and care on the son who was lost. He didn't understand it. How could his father do all of this for a son who had been disobedient and squandered his assets?

As he approached his father about what was happening, he began to share the things that he did "right" and the things the other son did wrong.

> *Then he became angry and didn't want to go in. So his father came out and pleaded with him. But he replied to his father, "Look, I have been slaving many years for you, and I have never disobeyed your orders, yet you never gave me a goat so that I could celebrate with my friends. But when this son of yours came, who has devoured your assets with prostitutes, you slaughtered the fattened calf for him."* (LUKE 15:28–30)

What the son maybe did not realize is that the comparison he brought to his father, explaining why his brother did not deserve what the father was giving him, was from a self-righteous place. As we walk with brothers and sisters overtaken in any sin, we must be careful to not compare ourselves. Making statements about what you would or would not have done or even about what this person does or doesn't deserve can be discouraging.

As the apostle Paul addresses the church of Galatia, he comes to a point where he teaches them how to carry one another's burdens. In this passage we have a model for how to walk with someone who is overtaken in any sin. Galatians 6:1–5 directs us:

> *Brothers and sisters, if someone is overtaken in any wrongdoing, you who are spiritual, restore such a person with a gentle spirit, watching out for yourselves so that you also won't be tempted. Carry one another's burdens; in this way you will fulfill the law of Christ. For if anyone considers himself to be something when he is nothing, he deceives himself. Let each person examine his own work, and then he can take pride in himself alone, and not compare himself with someone else. For each person will have to carry his own load.*

I love the look of restored antique furniture. If you've ever restored furniture, you understand that it's a delicate process. You sand off a layer of what's there before you begin to add new paint. But even as you paint the piece, you won't fully eliminate some of the knicks or scratches; the item will never look perfectly new. This is what helps give that piece of furniture character and what makes it stand out from something you picked up at Ikea.

As God uses us to restore others, it must be done in a similar way. It is done with a "gentle spirit," which means we help people walk in the newness of Christ in a caring manner. Our restoration does not involve dumbing down truth or accountability.

We aren't looking for perfection from this person, because only Jesus is perfect. We are patient with others as we help them walk out their repentance, being careful not to allow ourselves to be tempted as well. This is the restorative work in the body of Christ that brings God glory. As we work to restore a brother or sister in Christ, let us examine ourselves, knowing that it is by God's grace we are not in the same space.

Relationship Matters

I once heard about a Christian leader who had stepped out of public life for a time of renewal. People who knew nothing about the individual personally felt compelled to make unsolicited comments online about what might be going on behind the scenes with this person or their family. In light of the many negative and judgmental comments, I found myself thinking, *I really hope that this person has close relationships with others to surround them with encouragement and prayer.*

This made me think of when and how we should step in to a Galatians 6:1 situation. Is it fruitful to attempt to correct those who have fallen into sin that we have no relational capital with? I'm sure our attempts to admonish those online we are not connected with aren't reflective of the gentle restoration Christ has called us to.

I want to challenge us to take another stance when we see these instances. Instead of posting a praying hands emoji and quickly forgetting, we can pause and pray for that individual. Pray that they have genuine relationships with people in their lives who are there to walk out Galatians 6:1–5 with them. Pray that they are humbled to receive whatever correction the Lord brings their way and that they truly repent to the Lord and those they have hurt.

We must remember that the Lord is filled with joy any time a sinner repents and a person is restored. "But we had to celebrate and rejoice, because this brother of yours was dead and is alive again; he was lost and is found" (Luke 15:32). As we pray for our brothers and sisters, let us also rejoice with the Lord when we witness restoration taking place. Let us rejoice as we witness a renewed passion for the Lord. Let us rejoice when those who were once lost are now found.

> :: **TAKE A MOMENT**
>
> Where do you find yourself in the parable of the lost son? Are you in a prodigal place in need of restoration? Are you like the father and need to lovingly walk with someone in their restorative process? Or are you the older son, wrestling with self-righteousness?

6

Manifest

TRY TYPING THE WORD "MANIFEST" into TikTok. What do you see? I bet you see what I do: thousands of videos of people sharing how they "manifested" their dream life, or people coaching others on how they can manifest their desires.

What Is "Manifesting"?

Many of these coaches share how manifestation begins with your thoughts, which will cause you to actively visualize what you desire. Coupled with the right affirmations, you then should be able to "manifest" your desires into your life.

Some coaches take their manifestation instructions a step further by including different spells as they speak their intentions and desires. People will try anything to get what they want, from speaking their desires into a glass of water, to consulting tarot cards, to using specific crystals to manifest different things or to improve their manifestation powers. These approaches clearly take from a New Age line of thought and are touched by dark spiritual forces that Christians should have nothing to do with.[1]

If this is the use of "manifest" we hear from the world, it could be troubling to also hear this word from the church. Because its usage is incorrectly intertwined with Scripture (which replaces affirmations) or used with churchy lingo, it may be even more dangerous. The concept has seeped into various doctrines of the church that include "word of faith/prosperity gospel" movements and the "neo-prosperity gospel" movement.

Twisted truth is simply just a lie. And I'm afraid that many of us have fallen into the lie of manifestation culture and have been harmed by all that it implies.

Hard Days

"I lost my job." These words came from my husband's mouth early in our marriage.

Before we got married, both of us had been laid off from our jobs, but two weeks before the wedding, we landed new positions. We had seen God's favor in that area and just knew that we were going to be on a path of upward mobility. So to hear Jeff come home and tell me that he had lost his job when things were supposed to be "moving on up" in our lives hit me like a ton of bricks.

We were finally climbing out of some debt and caught up on the mortgage and other bills. We were actively serving in leadership in our church, and we were tithing members of the congregation. We also participated in what was called a Super Sunday offering where every person was to give one thousand dollars on top of our tithes to contribute toward a building project for the church.

As many of our peers prepared to give, some borrowed money to participate, or took out of savings. Others had yard sales to earn the requested offering amount. At the time we did whatever we could to give to this special offering. We were told of the special anointing on this offering to "break the back of lack." We heard testimonies of healing and open doors from people giving to this offering. As leaders it was made clear that we were to lead by example, which put extra pressure on us to make sure we did just that. Thousands of dollars were collected in these offerings.

During the services, people would line up and announce what they were giving followed by a declaration of faith and expectant praise. We had given into these offerings several times over and had checked all of the boxes of a faithful Christian couple.

I could not understand why this was happening to us.

Trying to Understand

As the days turned into weeks and weeks turned into months, I began to look at Jeff as if he must have been doing something wrong. "For you to be in this place, where is your faith?" I asked him. "Are you praying enough, Babe? What is it?"

I will never forget Jeff's response. "What if this is simply just God's will for me to walk through this right now?"

As I pondered that, I could not understand how God could be allowing this in our lives. A season of insurmountable debt due to unemployment surely had to come straight from Satan. We had tithed, even participated in all the special offerings, served faithfully, and confessed faith declarations over our lives daily. Our home was filled with declarative statements and vision boards followed by Scripture that we spoke over these visions every day.

My vision board included the titles of books I wanted to write someday, my dream house and car, pictures of families that appeared to be happy and thriving, along with other personal goals for our lives. There is nothing inherently wrong or sinful about a vision board. It is wise to have plans. Yet we become unwise when we aren't humbly surrendering these plans and visions to the will of God.

During this time we prayed earnestly, decreeing and declaring that God would answer our prayers because of the power we were taught that we had as believers. We were taught that we were made in the image of God, which is true, but we were also taught that we were little gods. This meant that our words must have had creative, supernatural power when spoken "in faith."

After a year of doing all the things that we thought we were supposed to do and not seeing any movement, we began to get discouraged. The way we were taught to exercise our faith was not working. We knew God was real and we had experienced Him operate in and through our lives. We both experienced the transformation that happens to us through our salvation.

I was beginning to have some doubts, though. When you've done all that you know to do in the "name of Jesus," and you've decreed and declared statements of faith repeatedly, and you remain in a place of unanswered prayer—it is dangerous what that may do to our view of who God truly is.

Misguided Notions

Where did this line of thinking originate?

We were taught the "word of faith" in our church. This teaching tells us that our faith had the power to produce good health and wealth into our lives. Our faith and our confessions over our faith was the main ingredient to have a prosperous life. Of course we needed to do our part, such as taking care of our bodies and maintaining good financial stewardship. But if we had sowed into our church, which was said to be "good ground," and decreed that we would receive wealth, then surely financial wealth would be our portion, and we would obtain victory in every area of our life.

Yes, the Scriptures promise treasures in heaven, but we were taught that we are entitled to experience heaven here on earth as well.

So when we experienced hard days in life such as loss of income, miscarriages, cancer diagnoses, and unexpected death in our family, we began to look at ourselves. What were we doing wrong? Were we not speaking the right Scriptures over our situations? Were we not saying the right words? Were these occurrences a result of sin or a lack of faith and belief in our lives?

What we would soon learn is that the experience of "suffering" had nothing to do with us or our lack of faith.

In the Lord's magnificent grace, He would begin to reveal to us His true nature and who we are in relation to His sovereignty. This understanding would feel like a warm, comforting blanket that relaxed our shoulders, unclenched our jaws, and dried our tears. In other words, the pressure was lifted.

Unfortunately, that didn't happen right away.

How about you? Have you sat under this type of teaching? Have you been confused when life didn't go as you expected even though you were doing and declaring the right things as you had been taught?

Over the years I have encountered countless people whose faith was adversely affected by their involvement in the Word of Faith movement. I think of Lauren, a mom and a wife who faithfully served and attended a Word of Faith ministry for five years. This ministry emphasized prophetic words above the Word of

God, encouraged its congregants to "name and claim" their blessings, and taught that they had the same power to control and shape their worlds by their words of faith.

At the time, Lauren and her family thought this expression of faith was biblical, but the Holy Spirit inside of her was beginning to prick her heart. She rarely received the personal prophetic words or the promised manifestations of health, wealth, or breakthrough. Because of this, she often wondered if God loved others more than He loved her, or if she simply lacked the faith that it took to receive these blessings over her life.

So she stepped up her works, committing to serving and praying even more. She begged God to speak to her as He did everyone else. The Lord began to answer her prayers in His way—by speaking to her as she explored how to study the Bible. This led her to teachers who expounded on the Scriptures in ways she never heard before, and she learned about the character of God.

A turning point came for her family during a sermon that was preached on a passage of Scripture that was explicitly about Christ; no one could miss it. Instead, the pastor centered the passage on self and left out the gospel altogether. This moment opened her eyes to a need for a theology rooted in truth, grounded in Scripture and not on personal gain.

Similar to Lauren, it took time for us to unravel the origins of this doctrine, which is the hallmark of the Word of Faith movement. Yet as the Lord would have it, our faith in Christ, along with a deep trust in the Lord's will, grew after learning truth. My heart for those who may read this and find themselves in this space is not to judge or condemn. I love and have relationships with many who remain under this doctrine. So, this chapter was difficult to write. My prayer is that it encourages the reader to take a deeper look into the origins of this doctrine and to pray, asking the Holy Spirit to reveal truth.

I also wrote this to release anyone of the shame of feeling like their works, faith declarations, and prayers simply weren't enough.

The Word of Faith Movement

The Word of Faith doctrine is present in churches and conferences all over the globe. Through cross-cultural services in various communities across the globe, I would see billboards advertising conferences promising to activate wealth, health, and victory through faith. I could understand how some who lived in poverty may be especially drawn to these events that promised to give them a formula to change their situation.

I could relate deeply to the appeal of a doctrine that told me that I could form my own world through my words and attract—or manifest—what I desired by my confessions of faith. Who wouldn't want that type of control?

In my early twenties, living in a community ravaged by poverty and violence, I was enticed by the promises of a lifestyle of ease and access. I encountered many Word of Faith pastors who were a picture of success but had not been born into wealth. When pastors reminisced of their humble beginnings and now demonstrated how they were experiencing the best of everything life had to offer, I, along with millions of others, wanted to know the way.

How had this doctrine that strayed so far away from orthodox Christianity come about? And let's be clear: This is not a doctrine or movement supported by Scripture or historic Christianity. E. W. Kenyon, a pastor and radio evangelist, is known as the founder of the Word of Faith movement. Kenyon was heavily influenced through New Thought, a movement that came out of Christian Science, which is also a false teaching. One of the teachings of New Thought was that "people shaped their own worlds by their thinking, just as God had created the world using thought. Positive thoughts yielded positive circumstances, and negative thoughts yielded negative situations."[2]

Kenyon took what he learned from New Thought theology and combined it with aspects of Christianity. This is called syncretism, "the attempt to combine different or opposite doctrines and practices, especially in reference to philosophical and religious systems."[3] We often see this today when people attempt to merge divination practices like astrology and tarot readings with Christianity.

E. W. Kenyon encouraged Christians to speak positive words that he called "positive confessions." A common quote of Kenyon's that is seen throughout the teachings of Word of Faith doctrine today is, "Faith never rises above its confession." Kenyon also taught that through prayer and the use of the name of Jesus we can have what we say.

> *Prayer took on binding legal qualities as believers followed Jesus' formula: "If ye shall ask anything in my name, I will do it" (John 14:14). Kenyon replaced the word "ask" with "demand," since petitioners were entitled to the legal benefits of Jesus' name. The Holy Spirit became merely an assistant as Kenyon gave the credit for casting out demons, speaking in tongues, and curing disease to the rightful use of the name of Jesus.* [4]

These ideas were later adopted by other Word of Faith teachers like Kenneth Erwin Hagin, Kenneth Copeland, and Benny Hinn. Hagin even became known as the father of the Word of Faith Movement. It was through his Bible institute, the Rhema Bible Training Center, publications, books, and radio broadcast that this message began to spread rapidly into communities of faith all over the United States. This drastically impacted how many Christian communities viewed themselves and God. A sovereign God became likened to a genie in a bottle or vending machine, ready to divvy out on our authority whatever we desired. This dangerous doctrine took the biblical truth that we are created in the image of God (which means we are to reflect His character and nature) and taught that we have the same abilities as God.

Prosperity Theology and Neo-Prosperity

In *Blessed*, Kate Bowler describes how prosperity theology is supposed to work:

> *Prosperity theology claims a power rooted in the operation of faith. Believers conceptualize faith as a causal agent, a power that actualizes events and objects in the real world. Faith acts as a force that reaches through the boundaries of materiality and into the spiritual realms, as if plucking objects from there and drawing them back into space and time.*[5]

Our faith is not meant to be used as a superpower that allows us to make things happen. It is an agent of trust and surrender given to us by the Holy Spirit. Even our salvation, which is the ultimate act of faith, is something that we cannot boast upon because it is a gift from God given to us. "For you are saved by grace through faith, and this is not from yourselves; it is God's gift—not from works, so that no one can boast" (Eph. 2:8–9).

Today the prosperity gospel movement looks different on the surface from the messages that flooded the church and airwaves during the '70s through the early 2000s. Gone are the days of being able to identify prosperity gospel pastors by the outward appearance of expensive three-piece suits, gator shoes, or preaching from various pulpits that "money cometh" to me.

The prosperity gospel teachers of today aren't typically found on infomercials promoting special anointing oil or prayer cloths that will help you manifest your desires. Because we don't see this type of faith teacher as much does not mean they aren't in churches, hosting conferences and workshops, and on social media. What we hear today from neo-prosperity gospel teachers is a self-help gospel. Like the traditional prosperity gospel movement, it also focuses on our ability to get the things we desire from God through activating our faith to receive what we perceive as promises from God. They tend to lump all the good things we desire as promises of God.

We may not hear the "money cometh" phrases of the traditional prosperity gospel movement often, but today's prosperity teachers continue to teach its followers to declare and decree what they desire by faith because a person's words have the ability to bring things to pass or to cancel things. This teaching is often backed by a verse in Proverbs: "Death and life are in the power of the tongue, and those who love it will eat its fruit" (18:21).

This wisdom given to us in Proverbs is a reminder that our words have consequences. Our words can lift situations and people up or tear them down. They can be used for destruction, or they can be used to glorify God. Our words cannot twist God's will to bend toward our desires. This is why Jesus models how we are to view our desires in light of God's will. Consider His words in the garden:

> *Going a little farther, he fell facedown and prayed, "My Father, if it is possible, let this cup pass from me. Yet not as I will, but as you will."* (MATT. 26:39)

In Jesus' humanity, as He weighed the journey before Him that would include immense physical and mental suffering, He asked if it was possible for this cup to pass from Him, if there was another way to salvation.

Jesus, being God in the flesh, at that moment could have said, "Father, this cup must pass and I cannot take this a step further; it's too painful." Instead, we see Christ in one of the most vulnerable moments of His human life cry out to God in agony and surrender His own will to the Father's. The will of God at that moment would include suffering. In *Surprised by Suffering*, R. C. Sproul shares,

> *Jesus qualified His prayer: "If it be thy will..." Jesus did not "name it and claim it." He knew His Father well enough to understand that it might not be His will. The story does not end with the words, "And the Father repented of the evil He had planned, removed the cup, and Jesus lived happily ever after." Such words border on blasphemy. The gospel is not a fairy tale. The Father would not negotiate the cup. Jesus was called to drink it to its last dregs. And He accepted it. "Nevertheless, not My will, but Yours, be done"* (LUKE 22:42).[6]

There is another line of thought within prosperity gospel movements that says we have the power to speak things into existence. These words are constantly heard within New Age culture and in churches across America. The verse that is used to substantiate that claim is: "As it is written: I have made you the father of many nations—in the presence of the God in whom he believed, the one who gives life to the dead and calls things into existence that do not exist" (Rom. 4:17).

Now, if we read this verse closely and within its context, we will see that Paul was referring to Yahweh—God as the One who gives life to the dead and calls things into existence from nothing. From the beginning God was the one who could say, "'Let there be light,' and there was light" (Gen. 1:3).

Yes, we are to have faith. We are to speak and pray God's words. But we do this with the heart of Jesus that humbly reminds us "If it be Your will."

There is no room in the prosperity gospel movements of yesterday and neo-prosperity gospel movements of today for the possibility that the will of God may not look as we desire it to. The will of God for our lives is often not the straight path we want or prefer with little to no pushback or suffering. If it were up to me, after I had gotten saved and given my life to the Lord, and since I had walked in sexual purity and waited for my husband, who was also pure—we would have gotten married, had a baby the following year, both walked into our dream careers that allowed us to give lots of money to the work of the kingdom and lived happily ever after in Christ.

> *"What happens when . . . ?" Is He not still Lord over these things?*

I wish it were that easy. As you read in previous chapters, it was not. Like a long road trip across the country, life is going to be filled with detours, rough terrain, smooth cruising moments, and times where we question the entire journey. Even through it all, the Lord is determined to receive all glory.

Believing that we have control and the ability to manifest our desires is a recipe for disaster when what we desire does not come to pass. What happens to our Jesus when we have spoken a desire in His name and we are not healed? What happens to our Jesus when, after praying for someone's healing, the person still passes away? What happens to our Jesus when it seems like every door is shut, the bills begin to pile up, and the job market is not in your favor? What happens to our Jesus if I never get married or have a child? What happens to our Jesus if I am still living with a chronic disease despite earnest prayers? What happens to our Jesus if the child I prayed for is born with a disability?

Is He not still Lord over these things? If our Jesus is connected simply to what He can do for us, then our relationship is transactional and conditional. This is an insult to our Jesus who has given us everything! Christ has already given us so much through the gift of the gospel, which gives us access to Him through the Holy Spirit. We must ask ourselves: If another prayer is not answered in the way that I expect or in the timing that I desire, will I still trust Him to be Lord, ruler over my life?

I must acknowledge there are times that trusting Him to be Lord and ruler over our lives is not easy. So I don't ask these questions from a place of having figured it out or having gotten it right all the time. Oftentimes, I am asking through tears, "Lord, what are You doing? I believe, but Lord, help my unbelief!" Jesus meets us in the tension of answered prayer and prayers still to be answered.

As the Jews were praying for a savior, a king who would establish His kingdom and free them from the bondage of the Romans, Jesus showed up. He didn't show up in the way many of them expected, but He was there. He dwelled among them, teaching them the way of the kingdom. When He ascended to the Father, He promised the Holy Spirit who would not only walk with us but serve as a Comforter who leads and guides believers into all truth. Day by day and at times moment by moment we have epiphanies of understanding only the Holy Spirit can reveal. The Holy Spirit is here, drawing us to focus more on the Giver than the gift.

Finding Comfort in the Sovereignty of God

When my father passed, my mother came to live with us. This season was beautifully hard. Beautiful because my mom and I were able to grieve together and comfort each other as we both took in this monumental loss. Hard because, well, grieving the loss of a loved one is always difficult. There was a lot to process during this transition, but it was beautiful being able to go through this this time with my mother.

As we began this stage of bereavement, I could tell my mother was extremely heavy in her spirit. Rightfully so; she and my father had been together for almost forty years. He was the love of her life. Yet in our conversations, I learned that she wrestled with wondering if she had not prayed the right words or prayed enough to keep him from dying. I understood how my mother could feel that way because I too struggled with the thought of "What could I have done to change this outcome?" At the time, we didn't have a solid understanding of the sovereignty of God.

As one commentator puts it, "God's sovereignty is his exercise of rule (as 'sovereign' or 'king') over his creation."[7] Our exclamation that "God is in control" is not based on conditions. He is in control while we are making our plans and decisions. He is ultimately in control as ruler over His creation. This does not mean that He's created humans to be His puppets. As a part of His divine rule, God has given His creation a will to make choices and decisions. However, our freedom does not make us "omnipotent," which means "all powerful." Our freedom of choice is in the confines of God's will. As we plan, pray, and seek to use our free will to glorify Christ, we can rest knowing that He is ultimately guiding our decisions.

> *A person's heart plans his way,*
> *but the LORD determines his steps.* (PROV. 16:9)

*Many plans are in a person's heart,
but the Lord's decree will prevail.* (PROV. 19:21)

*A king's heart is like channeled water in the Lord's hand:
He directs it wherever he chooses.* (PROV. 21:1)

What a comforting thought to know that as we plan our ways, the Lord is ordering our steps! As we go about our lives, what we experience isn't a surprise to our sovereign King. Now, you may be wondering if God is so sovereign, then did He kill my friend or did He give my mother cancer or did He give my child this chronic illness? Then we would have to also ask ourselves, Is this in line with the character of God? Although His power is infinite, will He do things that are not within His character? We can trust that "God cannot will or do anything that would deny his own character. Thus, God cannot lie, sin, deny himself, or be tempted with evil. He cannot cease to exist, or cease to be God, or act in a way inconsistent with any of his attributes."[8] It's also comforting to know that since God is in control, He can work people's sinful choices for our good and use the situation for His glory.

We know that all things work together for the good of those who love God, who are called according to his purpose. (ROM. 8:28)

:: **TAKE A MOMENT**

Reflect on a moment in your life when the Lord used what was a horrible or challenging situation for your good. Think of Joseph. His brothers who were jealous of him sold him into slavery and lied to their father, Jacob, about what happened to him. They never expected to see him again.

> Yet the Lord kept Joseph, blessing him with gifts that kept him until he eventually became a ruler in Egypt. (Read the story in Genesis 37–50.) What is your Joseph story?

We may not always understand why something is happening the way it has. We may find ourselves asking often, "Lord, why do I have to walk this route? Why am I experiencing this particular roadblock?" In our questions, may we take comfort in the truth that God's sovereignty protects and keeps the saints until the end of time.

Characteristics of God We Can—and Cannot—Imitate

Is God like us? Are we like God? The answers may seem obvious, but let's discuss them.

It is no secret that we are all born into sin and have a propensity toward particular sins we may wrestle with. We have all fallen short of the glory of God and need the saving grace of Jesus Christ that redeems us. No matter what sins we have committed or struggle with today, this is the truth that links humans more than anything.

The one who is not like us is God. There is no sin in Him, "absolutely no darkness in him" (1 John 1:5).

But because we have been made in His image, there are some character traits that we can model. These are called "communicable" attributes. The attributes of God that we can imitate are things like His love, mercy, peace, justice, and holiness. Being created in His image, with the help of the Holy Spirit, we can imitate the God we experience. Scripture doesn't merely suggest that we imitate God but commands it: "Therefore, be imitators of God, as dearly loved children, and walk in love, as Christ also loved us and gave himself for us, a sacrificial and fragrant offering to God" (Eph. 5:1–2).

As we freely experience His unconditional love, may we freely give His unconditional love. As we freely experience His mercy and grace, may we extend that mercy and grace to others.

Nonetheless, there are attributes of God's character that we cannot imitate. These attributes are what makes God different from us—which is a good thing! These are the characteristics that make God, God. They are called incommunicable attributes. Incommunicable attributes are those characteristics that God does not share with His creation.

God doesn't change: "Jesus Christ is the same yesterday, today, and forever" (Heb. 13:8). Unlike Him, we are always changing. We grow older and mature. Our health changes. Not only do we change appearances consistently, but our perspectives and attitudes are always changing as we evolve and have different experiences.

God is eternal, which means He has existed before time and will exist for all eternity. He is not bound by time as we are. Revelation 1:8 tells us,

> "I am the Alpha and the Omega," says the Lord God, "the one who is, who was, and who is to come, the Almighty."

Our existence begins at our conception. Our days on earth are numbered. Scripture tells us, "All my days were written in your book and planned before a single one of them began" (Ps. 139:16). So like the psalmist may we pray, "Teach us to number our days carefully so that we may develop wisdom in our hearts" (Ps. 90:12). We pray this knowing that our eternal God who is not bound by time may help us make the most of our time and receive the glory out of every area of our lives.

God is omnipresent, which means He is present everywhere at once. You know the church saying, "He may not come when you want Him, but He's right on time." Cue the organ! Well, if God is truly omnipresent, that means He is always there, all the time.

> *Where can I go to escape your Spirit?*
> *Where can I flee from your presence?*
> *If I go up to heaven, you are there;*
> *if I make my bed in Sheol, you are there.*
> *If I fly on the wings of the dawn and*
> *settle down on the western horizon,*
> *even there your hand will lead me;*
> *your right hand will hold on to me.* (PS. 139:7–10)

Even when we don't "feel" like He's here, He's here. He's here in our suffering; He is present through our tears. He is there during our highest and lowest moments. Although in our shame, we clothe ourselves with fig leaves to attempt to hide from His presence, we cannot escape Him. "There is nowhere in the entire universe, on land or sea, in heaven or hell, where one can flee from God's presence."⁹

> *We can trust that Christ will manifest what needs to be in our lives and in the perfect timing.*

Our God is not limited; He cannot be boxed in to our finite human minds. This is who we trust as the One who manifests. He calls things into existence; He speaks, and things appear. We can trust that Christ will manifest what needs to be in our lives and in the perfect timing. Christ being eternal means that there is an eternal view that we aren't able to see. Yet we live in light of eternity, knowing that one glorious day everything will be made right when the Lord comes for His church. There is a future glory that will be revealed.

And until that day, we trust, in faith, that the Lord will bring to pass His perfect will for our lives.

7

Promises

> *For every one of God's promises is "Yes" in him.*
> *Therefore, through him we also say "Amen" to the glory of God.*
>
> 2 CORINTHIANS 1:20

WHAT ARE THE PROMISES OF God? This was a question I often asked as I sat during years of infertility. In an attempt to encourage my faith, some people would tell me that it was a promise of God to open my womb. But was that really true?

Yes and Amen

Yes, after eleven years the Lord did allow me to conceive, so that particular prayer was answered. But does that mean that fertility is a promise from God for all women who desire it? I often heard 2 Corinthians 1:20 paraphrased as "all of God's promises are Yes and Amen" and being used as a blanket statement to mean that the promises of God are the things that we desire. For years I believed our desire for marriage, children, physical healing, wealth, and more are all a promise of God and therefore we can rest knowing that God *will* do these things for us.

Nonetheless, as we discussed in the previous chapter, this is simply not how God works. His promises for us today are indeed real. God keeps His promises, and these promises are even greater and more fulfilling than our personal desires.

Before Paul arrives at this statement in 2 Corinthians 1:20, he speaks about the God who comforts. Paul was no stranger to suffering, having experienced persecution throughout his various missionary journeys. His letter to the church in Corinth encouraged the saints to stand firm in their faith. A part of standing firm would include knowing who God is in the midst of their sufferings. We share in Christ's sufferings, but we also share in His comfort: "For just as the sufferings of Christ overflow to us, so also through Christ our comfort overflows" (2 Cor. 1:5).

Paul doesn't make light of suffering and shares about being "overwhelmed—beyond our strength—so that we even despaired of life itself" (2 Cor. 1:8). Isn't that relatable? Unanswered prayer can simply be overwhelming beyond our strength.

While waiting for the Lord to bless you with a spouse, you may feel like your biological clock is ticking. When praying for a child to surrender their lives to the Lord, you may feel like you've done all you can do. When you feel like you're a slave to debt and can't see a way out, you may feel trapped. When you're doing all you can to fight a disease and the test results remain the same.... These types of things can cause you to despise the life you are in and despair that your situation will ever change. Trusting in ourselves just won't do it. Paul tells the church we must place our trust in the God who raises the dead. We place our trust in someone who has the power to do what we cannot.

As this chapter of Scripture continues, Paul seeks to give a reason for postponing one of his visits. Deviating from his announced plans, "Paul made a brief, painful visit from Ephesus to Corinth, and then returned to Ephesus. Some believers in Corinth accused him of being unreliable and purely human. The charge of saying Yes, yes one minute and No, no the next stung him into reacting defensively."[1] He shares that he and Timothy were not being unreliable and sought to communicate God's reliability in the next verse:

> As God is faithful, our message to you is not "Yes and no." For the Son of God, Jesus Christ, whom we proclaimed among you—Silvanus, Timothy, and I—did not become "Yes and no." On the contrary, in him it is always "Yes." For every one of God's promises is "Yes" in him. Therefore, through him we also say "Amen" to the glory of God. (2 COR. 1:18–20)

This gives us context for this verse that speaks to God's promises. We can rejoice knowing that all of God's promises are yes in Him, and we say "amen," which means "so be it" and seals the deal.

Examining the Promises

Paul, being an avid student of the law, is referring to Old Testament promises. Research estimates that there are more than 8,000 promises made in the Bible, with over 7,400 of them being promises made by God to humankind.[2] It's important to note that these promises can be categorized as general (applicable to all believers) or specific (made to particular individuals in certain contexts), and discernment is needed to understand which promises apply in different situations. Of course, we cannot discuss every promise of God in this book, but I do want us to think critically about how we can read these promises and make a decision on how they do or do not apply to us today.

Let's take Jeremiah 33:14–15 as an example:

> *"Look, the days are coming"—this is the LORD's declaration—"when I will fulfill the good promise that I have spoken concerning the house of Israel and the house of Judah. In those days and at that time I will cause a Righteous Branch to sprout up for David, and he will administer justice and righteousness in the land."*

Jeremiah prophesied this promise to the people of Judah during their exile; we talked about the Babylonian exile and judgment due to their sin. Jeremiah was speaking of the coming of Christ, the Righteous Branch, who will rise through the line of David. This promise was for this group of people during a particular time in history, but there are biblical principles we can pull from this passage:

- God doesn't abandon people in their moments of suffering or pain.
- God loves us through whatever trial we are experiencing, always giving us an answer in Jesus!
- And although Christ fulfilled this promise here in Jeremiah 33:14–15 through His coming, we can also have hope for His future coming: "Christ, having been offered once to bear the sins of many, will appear a second time, not to bear sin, but to bring salvation to those who are waiting for him" (Heb. 9:28).

Even if it is a promise that does not directly apply to us since we are not exiled in Babylon, because all Scripture is inspired by the Holy Spirit, there is always truth that we can grasp.

> *For whatever was written in the past was written for our instruction, so that we may have hope through endurance and through the encouragement from the Scriptures.* (ROM. 15:4)

> *All Scripture is inspired by God and is profitable for teaching, for rebuking, for correcting, for training in righteousness, so that the man of God may be complete, equipped for every good work.* (2 TIM. 3:16–17)

The entire counsel of God is for our instruction, points us to hope, and helps us endure until the coming of Christ.

Critical Thinking

As we learn to think critically and discern which promises are to all believers or instead to specific groups of people in Scripture, it's important that we explore how to interpret Scripture. Growing up, I was often told that the Bible is the greatest love story of all that shows us just how much the Lord loves His creation. While that statement does have some truth, the Bible should not be minimized to be some rom-com of Jesus chasing us down to save us.

The Bible is a book about God, His character, and His plan for humanity. It shares how humanity has fallen short due to sin and continues to fall short throughout history. It shows that although we are created as image bearers, our sin keeps us out of true fellowship with God. The Scriptures detail humanity's need for a Savior as men and women, kings and prophets, consistently miss the mark. Finally, we are reminded of the future glory and hope we have as people who truly are in this world but not of it. Scripture's ancient writings are inspired by the Holy Spirit and written in different genres. All of this must be considered as we seek to interpret what we are reading and learn what applies to us today.

Genres of Scripture

The Bible is broken down into different types of genres: Law/Historical, Old Testament Narrative, Poetry, Wisdom, Prophecy, Gospels, Letters/Epistles, and Apocalyptic. Reading and studying the Bible with this information before us can help with how we apply Scripture to our lives. For example, the way we would read to understand a book of poetry by Nikki Giovanni or Langston Hughes would be different from how we would read a narrative about the life of Frederick Douglass.

So yes, if we want to truly understand what God is saying throughout the Bible, it is helpful to pull out some of our grade school English skills because each book is a beautiful piece of literature written in a specific genre. Knowing these genres is helpful within our inductive Bible study and helps us to know how and what to apply. I'm appreciative of Kristie Anyabwile's insights in her book *Literarily: How Understanding Bible Genres Transforms Bible Study* that I cite in this section.

The Law

The Law books, also known as the Pentateuch or Torah, are the first five books in the Bible: Genesis, Exodus, Leviticus, Numbers, and Deuteronomy. Throughout the law we read narratives, which are written accounts of stories about Adam and Eve, Moses, Joshua, Abraham and Sarah, Isaac, Rebekah, Jacob, and many others, often derived from oral accounts. We are able to read about these people's shortcomings, victories, and ultimately their need for God. We read why and how the law was established, which was to guide God's people, while providing instructions on how to live a holy life.

We consistently read time and time again about the people of God who simply couldn't or wouldn't perfectly obey the laws He put in place. Kristie Anyabwile puts it like this: "We need the law not only to show us the problem of sin but also to lead us to the only solution for our sin problem, the Lord Jesus Christ and the deliverance He promises for those who repent of their sins and trust in Him."[3]

So what does this mean for how we interpret the law books today? Consider this verse: "Everything in the water that does not have fins and scales will be abhorrent to you" (Lev. 11:12).

If I read those words without an understanding of the type of book I was reading, I would be upset and thoroughly confused. I just happen to live in the great state of Maryland, famous for the Maryland blue crab. There is absolutely nothing like gathering with family or friends on a summer day and sitting and cracking blue crabs, topped with Old Bay seasoning, some melted butter on the side, along with some steamed spiced shrimp. Why did the law of Moses prohibit this? We might not understand the reasons for all the regulations, but we can see that the Lord was interested in every aspect of our lives and wanted every part of us to be holy to Him.

In fact, in the Old Testament there are laws against eating pork, having piercings, and wearing garments of clothing that are made up of more than one fabric. If people disobeyed these laws, whether dietary or ceremonial, they were considered unclean.

I often wondered why God established these laws that He knew the people would ultimately have challenges keeping. "God does not want them to be like the nations around them who did not know or worship God. He wanted His people to stand out, set apart for Him. From their inward attitudes to their outward behavior, the Israelites were to be a people marked by holiness so all the nations would know they worshiped the one true God."[4]

Case Study

Joshua 1:3 says, "I have given you every place where the sole of your foot treads, just as I have promised to Moses."

I've seen churches and individuals that will go to a potential property and pray this Scripture over the land, believing that the Lord will give them this particular land as their foot treads over it.

But before we're quick to claim this promise as our own, we must look at who this promise was being communicated to and why. The Lord was reminding Joshua that the promised land that He'd first promised Moses and that they had just entered into was already theirs.

In reading this verse, we are not being promised any land we want. But we are being challenged to see who God is in the passage and how He relates to people like us.

What we see demonstrated here, and what we learn about ourselves, is that even in God's sovereignty, we have a responsibility to step out in faith when God calls us to do something.

Just as He promised to bring the children of Israel into the promised land, so He has fulfilled His promise of sending us a Savior and will continue to fulfill every promise related to the ongoing process of our redemption and restoration.

History/Old Testament Narrative

Most of the Old Testament contains narratives. These stories give us a glimpse of real people experiencing real things. The Old Testament historical narratives can possibly compete with some of your favorite modern reality television shows. It gets a bit dicey and juicy in some areas.

However, we aren't just reading biblical "tea" or gossip. These situations teach us the conditions of humans, our victories, our problems and how we attempt to solve them, the many sinful choices and mistakes made, and our consistent need for a Savior. In narratives we learn from the biblical characters' victories and their errors. "The beauty of narratives is that they show rather than tell. The storyline (also called the plot) helps us discover what the story is emphasizing so we avoid improperly spiritualizing (looking for deeper spiritual meaning beyond what the text and context allow) or blindly contextualizing the narrative (bringing the text forward to our day too quickly)."[5]

As we read these historical narratives that detail the stories of many people, we must remember these stories rest in a larger framework that in some way will point us to Christ. This is called the "metanarrative," or the big picture of the Bible. The metanarrative is usually broken down into four parts: Creation, Disruption or Fall, Redemption, and Restoration. The Bible begins with the creation story in Genesis. God creates the heavens and the earth. He creates humans in His image and gives them dominion over creation. Yet due to their sin of disobedience in the garden of Eden we witness the fall of man. This is why we needed the person and work of Jesus Christ.

After Christ redeems creation to its original order and purpose, God dwells with humanity and lives with us (Rev. 21:3). Reading Scripture through this lens helps us be encouraged by God's promises to do exactly what He said He would do.

Case Study

"If . . . my people, who bear my name, humble themselves, pray and seek my face, and turn from their evil ways, then I will hear from heaven, forgive their sin, and heal their land" (2 Chron. 7:13–14).

This verse has been prayed in prayer meetings across the world. It is often applied in the context that if Christians would pray, humble ourselves, seek God's face, and turn from our evil ways, then the Lord will not only hear these prayers, but He will also forgive our sin and heal our nation.

There are truths from this verse that we can apply. But before we extract those, it's important to recognize the context in which this was written. The verse "refers to times when the Israelites have become faithless to God and are enduring the consequences, whether it was a famine, an invasion, or even the deportation to another country. To be humble . . . pray . . . seek God and turn from sin are four aspects of one attitude: repentance. If Israel would repent, he would forgive them and heal their spiritual relationship with him associated with the promised land."[6]

This promise is specific to God's covenant people; however, those who are under the new covenant can extract things about the nature of God through this verse:

- God desires His people to pray and seek Him in all things.
- God desires for His people to be humble. "Humble yourselves before the Lord, and he will exalt you" (James 4:10).
- He is a God who desires repentance of sin and is ready to forgive.
- He is gracious and merciful with the power to heal our land if it is His will.

This does not mean that this verse shouldn't be shared in a prayer meeting or even prayed. In fact, it's a beautiful verse to pray as we keep these things about God in mind, with an understanding of the original covenant God made to His people as we apply its principles in our relationship with Him.

Prophecy and Poetry

The prophetic books are broken down into what's called "major and minor" prophets. The major prophetic books are Isaiah, Jeremiah, Ezekiel, Daniel, and Lamentations. (Note: Lamentations is also filled with poetry.) The minor prophet books are Hosea, Joel, Amos, Obadiah, Jonah, Micah, Nahum, Habakkuk, Zephaniah, Haggai, Zechariah, and Malachi.

Throughout the prophetic books we are introduced to prophets whose primary role is to be a mouthpiece for God. These prophetic words were given to Israel as instructions and warnings. There are prophecies of judgment, calls for repentance, and hope for restoration. Israel and Judah have a complex history that is filled with disobedience and idolatry. In the prophetic books we read how God's people have gone astray and that there is only one King who can save them. Although they have chosen many kings throughout their history, history shows that these kings aren't sufficient and further points to the need of redemption through Jesus Christ.

As we read the prophetic books, there is wisdom we can gain even if these prophecies aren't directed toward us today. We must note that when we read a prophetic book in Scripture, the prophet is being called by God to give a specific word from Him to a group of people. This prophet is speaking to their situation, and many of these prophecies aren't directed toward us. Deep disappointment and even heresy can creep in if we don't realize this. Despite this, we can still gain wisdom and learn about the character of God and who He is.

Throughout the prophetic books we are able to see, through the words of various prophets to God's people, that there are consequences to our sin. As we study and read these prophecies, combing through the promises within them, may it help us to long for our coming King. May it prick our hearts as we rejoice because of the redemption and restoration that's available only through Christ.

Case Study

Let's take what I like to call a "bumper sticker" verse. It's one that is commonly seen on bumper stickers, T-shirts, journal covers, and more.

> "For I know the plans I have for you"—this is the LORD's declaration—"plans for your well-being, not for disaster, to give you a future and a hope." (JER. 29:11)

This verse is often used to encourage someone going through a difficult time. And I believe this verse can be and is incredibly encouraging for the believer. In quoting it, however, we can miss the full meaning of this verse if we don't look at the context. In Jeremiah 29:10, the Lord says when seventy years for Babylon are complete, He will begin this process of restoration. Seventy years?! Having an unanswered prayer for one year can be gut-wrenching, so I cannot imagine what the Jewish exiles were feeling, knowing they would have to wait seventy years to return to their own land.

Of course, there are some things we learn about God in this passage when we examine its context. First, we must take into account that these words are given by the prophet Jeremiah in a letter to remaining exiled elders, priests, prophets, and all the people King Nebuchadnezzar deported from Jerusalem to Babylon. Let's look at the verses prior to verse 11:

> This is what the LORD of Armies, the God of Israel, says to all the exiles I deported from Jerusalem to Babylon: "Build

houses and live in them. Plant gardens and eat their produce. Find wives for yourselves, and have sons and daughters. Find wives for your sons and give your daughters to men in marriage so that they may bear sons and daughters. Multiply there; do not decrease. Pursue the well-being of the city I have deported you to. Pray to the Lord on its behalf, for when it thrives, you will thrive." (JER. 29:4–7)

What do we learn about God in this passage? God wanted His people to flourish in the midst of hardship. While waiting for our prayers to be answered, we are not to cower and wither away. Now, our assignment may not be to build houses or find wives and have children. That was a specific word for the exiles in that place and time. But we can read this passage and see that God is challenging His people to be fruitful during this period of exile. During this difficult time and the long journey ahead of them He reminds them that He's all-knowing and that His plans are good. That's what we can hold on to about God in Jeremiah 29.

He knows whatever plans He has for us, and we can trust that they will be for His glory and our good. No matter what, we can hold on to the hope that's in Christ.

Poetry

The Bible often uses poetry to communicate its truths. We see this in Psalms, Job, Proverbs, Lamentations, and the Song of Solomon. We can also find passages of poetry throughout other parts of the Bible, such as in Jeremiah. Many of our worship songs come from these poetic passages and can be used to extol and praise God. They also can be used to give us words to bless or pray.

As for any poem, we must take note of the way it's written. We should also take note of the imagery in poetry, remembering we'll spot metaphors and symbolism throughout.

Case Study

Let's take this commonly quoted verse: "Weeping may stay overnight, but there is joy in the morning" (Ps. 30:5). The imagery here is in the use of the word "morning."

The truth is when there is sorrow, joy may not come in the actual morning. I can't tell you how many times a well-meaning person told me in my darkest hour that there will be joy in the morning. Many times, you may find yourself mourning a loss or a heartbreak for several mornings to come. "The morning often represents restoration or blessing in the psalms."[7] Therefore, as we read this psalm, we can be encouraged that the Lord will bring restoration. We may not know when it will come for our particular situation. We also don't know the day or the hour when Christ will come and restore all things back to Himself. But what we do know is that we serve a God who restores! And we can sing or pray that psalm joyfully, knowing that restoration is ours!

> :: **TAKE A MOMENT**
> What is your favorite psalm or verse from Proverbs? What imagery can you find in it? Write down any wisdom or truth that relates to the big picture of the Bible.

Gospels

Matthew, Mark, Luke, and John tell the "good news" of Jesus' life, His earthly ministry, His death, and resurrection. Both the Gospels and the letters fall into the redemption part of the metanarrative of Scripture.

Each gospel details certain aspects of the life of Christ. The words of Jesus are recorded throughout the Gospels as He teaches at various moments through parables or sermons. We also learn from Jesus' conversations with people He encountered on His journey, such as the woman at the well in John 4.

As we read and study the Gospels, it is helpful to know who the writer is of each particular one. One writer may be more compressed, while another may offer more detail. The Gospels are not merely biographical, but they are a survey of Jesus' ministry. What remains the same is that each writer draws on eyewitness accounts from His closest followers of what Jesus did and said. "We must therefore study them concentrating on the person of Jesus, and use all possible literary tools to see how each gospel writer composes his particular portrait."[8]

Letters

Oh, the joy I have when someone sends a card to our home—or even better, when I receive a letter! I cannot tell you the last time I received a letter in the mail. Okay, I am challenging myself to send a letter to someone! This form of communication is almost nonexistent in the world of emails and text messaging. The thoughtfulness and care it takes to write a letter is what we see in the epistles, which make up a third of the New Testament.

Though the promises written throughout the New Testament are for believers, we must also note that the letters were written to churches with specific backgrounds. This means some of the directives will be cultural, or specific to that time and place.

When reading and studying a letter it's important to not skip the introduction, since it tells us who the author is and who they are writing to. For example, what do we learn here?

> *Paul, an apostle of Christ Jesus by God's will and Timothy our brother. To the saints in Christ at Colossae, who are faithful brothers and sisters. Grace to you and peace from God our Father.* (COL. 1:1–2)

We see that this was written to Christians (faithful brothers and sisters) in the city of Colossae, which is now a part of modern-day Turkey, and it was from Paul and Timothy. When seeking to study and apply the truths in Colossians, we'd keep these facts in mind.

Many of the letters are pastoral in nature, giving us insight on the needs and challenges of various churches during that time. Some were written by Paul while he was in prison. Others were written by Peter, John, Jude, and James. "They were real people, like the readers of the Letters today. So each letter had a specific purpose, addressing the particular needs of the readers, which varies greatly from letter to letter."[9] As you read about the challenges and needs of these first-century churches, you will find many similarities to what we are experiencing today. False teaching, idolatry, paganism, and overall unfaithfulness to the gospel message were running rampant through the church. Although we are different culturally, our need to be redeemed by Christ remains the same.

Case Study

> *In him we have also received an inheritance, because we were predestined according to the plan of the one who works out everything in agreement with the purpose of his will, so that we who had already put our hope in Christ might bring praise to his glory.* (EPH. 1:11–12)

This verse is a part of a beautiful section in my Bible labeled, "God's Rich Blessings." These blessings are not in the form of material possessions. These rich blessings are spiritual. The inheritance that we are able to look forward to is the promised Holy Spirit. Although this letter was written to the faithful saints in Christ Jesus at Ephesus, if you are in Christ and part of His church, then these words are a promise to you too. Throughout this letter, Paul shares the gospel by breaking down who we are in Christ, our reconciliation, and redemption. These beautiful promises apply to every believer who has trusted Christ with their lives.

Apocalyptic Literature

As I mentioned earlier, when I was a child, I had a weird obsession with apocalyptic literature due to its eschatological nature. I had come across some books about end times, and they confused and rather upset me.

I don't believe this is what God intended when He inspired the writers to write the parts of the Bible that we term "apocalyptic." Instead, these books provided hope to first-century Christians and should provide hope to us for the restoration that is to come. When reading apocalyptic literature, such as what's found in Revelation and Daniel, we must realize that the symbolism and images are written to people in that era. These people were familiar with the Old Testament writings where we can find meanings for many of the symbols.

I am no expert in interpreting apocalyptic passages and am still considering my eschatological views today. One promise is helpful to remember though, especially if you are working through the pain of unanswered prayer: "All that God promised to Abraham and his descendants, the restoration He promised wayward Israel, the kingdom of God Jesus ushered in and taught the disciples, the ability to see God face to face and not die but live and worship Him eternally, the mortal taking on immortality—all of this comes to ultimate fulfillment in this last book of the Bible."[10]

What we see in Revelation, therefore, is not just a description of a singular apocalyptic event but a fulfillment of all God has promised.

All throughout Scripture within the historical narratives, prophetic books, and Gospels, we witness fallen people and their stories. Each story ultimately reveals one thing: We are in need of redemption. As we move through the Gospels, we come to the point of redemption. Only One is sent who can redeem this fallen world back to the right relationship with the Creator. As Jesus is prophesied, and as He enters the picture, we see how creation will be redeemed. Finally, the revelation that is given to the apostle John reveals God's plan for restoration:

> *Then I saw a new heaven and a new earth; for the first heaven and the first earth had passed away, and the sea was no more. I also saw the holy city, the new Jerusalem, coming down out of heaven from God, prepared like a bride adorned for her husband.* (REV. 21:1–2)

According to His Will

So yes, all of God's promises, the prophetic declarations to His coming and who He is throughout the Old Testament, are Yes. The fulfillment of who Christ is and what is to come is a hearty Amen! It's a finished work we can rejoice in. These are promises we can cling to while earnestly praying for His will to be done in every area of our life.

I also don't want to discourage the voice of God in our prayer life. There are times the Lord places a God-glorifying desire within our hearts that keeps us on our knees petitioning Him. I am sure that you can recount answered prayers in your life even if there is a list of prayers you are still waiting to receive answers on. All throughout Scripture we see God answering the prayers of His people. Have no doubt—God answers prayer and encourages us to pray. He wants us to have faith in Him and trust in His word. In John 14, Jesus says, "Whatever you ask in my name, I will do it so that the Father may be glorified in the Son. If you ask me anything in my name, I will do it" (vv. 13–14).

The apostle John shares this qualifier about our prayers: "This is the confidence we have before him: If we ask anything according to his will, he hears us. And if we know that he hears whatever we ask, we know that we have what we have asked of him" (1 John 5:14–15).

We can be confident that *God will answer prayer according to His will*. We do not change God's mind with our prayers or feed Him information we think He might not be aware of. He is all-knowing, all-wise, and completely good. He will do what is best. We can be confident in having our prayers answered when they line up with what God wants to happen.[11] So as we pray and discern God's promises to us, may we always be ready to surrender it to God's will.

∷ TAKE A MOMENT

Have you ever had a word of the year that you felt the Lord impress upon your heart to focus on? "Surrender" was my word of the year for several years. I believe it's because I had the most challenges surrendering my desires to whatever His will would be for my life. This is still a major challenge today. As you trust God to be God and as you work to take Him at His word, what is the unanswered prayer you need to surrender to Him? Write that here.

I'll let you in on mine: my mother's complete healing from metastatic breast cancer. I am surrendering this to the Lord. He is the only One who has the power to heal, and I trust Him to heal when and how He wants. May it all be for His glory. Amen.

8

Remember

> *When the LORD your God brings you into the land he swore to your ancestors Abraham, Isaac, and Jacob that he would give you—a land with large and beautiful cities that you did not build, houses full of every good thing that you did not fill them with, cisterns that you did not dig, and vineyards and olive groves that you did not plant—and when you eat and are satisfied, be careful not to forget the LORD who brought you out of the land of Egypt, out of the place of slavery.*
>
> DEUTERONOMY 6:10–12

> *If God's memory therefore records all that he has given me, let me be ashamed to let my memory suffer these things to slip. What God counts worthy of his divine recollection let me record on the pages of my memory, and often let me peruse the record.*—C. H. Spurgeon[1]

SOMETIMES I HAVE SELECTIVE MEMORY. How about you? This means we have a tendency to remember the things we want to remember.

Sometimes I need help remembering certain things, so I have to write them down in a journal, on my phone, or on a white board. This, combined with a real phenomenon called "mom brain" and coupled with being in my forties, that makes remembering things more challenging than it used to be. Experiencing the changes in my natural ability to remember has caused me to work on building my memory and cognition through things like word games, crossword puzzles, and more.

Memory is truly a gift from the Lord, but it can also feel like a curse when our memories are filled with difficulties. Living in this world, we all will experience good, sad, exciting, traumatic, and hard memories. And I've learned, for some reason, it feels easier to remember the things that have hurt or caused us pain. For others, it's easy to bury the memories or have dissociative amnesia for memories that are traumatic.

In this chapter we are going to talk about the power of remembering, what we should remember about God while walking through unanswered prayer, and how we can surrender these memories in ways that are healing to our souls.

Memorial Stones

I've always paid extra attention to the word "remember" while reading Scripture. When the Lord tells someone to remember something, it serves great purpose, and we can often learn from the types of things they were being commanded to remember. When the children of Israel crossed over the Jordan River into the land of Canaan, the Lord gave them instructions through His servant Joshua. Everything that the Lord would tell them to remember was related to who He is and what He had done for them. He didn't command them to remember their mistakes and how they failed many times. He didn't command them to remember their hardships in the wilderness.

He began by sharing with them the importance of remembering or "meditating" on the book of instruction: "This book of instruction must not depart from your mouth; you are to meditate on it day and night so that you may carefully observe everything written in it" (Josh. 1:8). Here we see the importance of remembering God's word. His words and instructions bring life and establish those who meditate on them. This word "meditate" is *hagah* in the Hebrew, which means to mutter, read in an undertone, speak, and proclaim. This verse gives us a tip on memorizing Scripture. It involves reading God's Word out loud to ourselves, repetitive reading, speaking, and proclaiming. Remembering Scripture anchors us in truth when the lies of the enemy attempt to overwhelm us or to simply lie about the character of God.

> ∷ **TAKE A MOMENT**
>
> When was the last time you memorized Scripture? I realized that while walking through loss and disappointment I needed more Scripture in my memory bank than what I learned as a child in Sunday school. What are you meditating on today that is anchoring you in truth? Use this moment to write down those specific verses and passages on a clean page in your journal. Commit to meditating on them daily as you anchor yourself with the truth of who God is.

The children of Israel had been through a lot during their forty-year journey through the wilderness and into the promised land. As they crossed the Jordan River, the Lord spoke to Joshua about how to remember this monumental journey. He tells Joshua to choose twelve men from the people, one to represent each of the twelve tribes, and to take twelve stones from the middle of the Jordan. These stones were to be carried and then set down at the place where they would spend the night. Throughout future generations, when children asked what the stones were for, they would learn that the stones were a reminder of when "'the water of the Jordan was cut off in front of the ark of the LORD's covenant. When it crossed the Jordan, the Jordan's water was cut off.' Therefore these stones will always be a memorial for the Israelites" (Josh. 4:7).

As they crossed the Jordan River on dry ground, they were to remember what Yahweh had done for them before as they crossed the Red Sea on dry ground. These stones were a memorial, a reminder that He is the same God who will continue to be with them. They were to remember the strength of the Lord so that they may revere Him always.

> Then Joshua set up in Gilgal the twelve stones they had taken from the Jordan, and he said to the Israelites, "In the future, when your children ask their fathers, 'What is the meaning of these stones?' you should tell your children, 'Israel crossed the Jordan on dry ground.' For the LORD your God dried up the water of the Jordan before you until you had crossed over, just as the LORD your God did to the Red Sea, which he dried up before us until we had crossed over. This is so that all the peoples of the earth may know that the LORD's hand is strong, and so that you may always fear the LORD your God." (JOSH. 4:20–24)

Raise an Ebenezer!

At the beginning of this chapter, I shared about my selective memory. I tend to remember the hard things more. It is truly not my finest quality. My husband often redirects me away from pessimism so that I will lean toward the truth of who God is. I remember how something made me feel, and if I'm not careful I will replay the pain of a situation on the canvas of my mind over and over again. Knowing this about myself, I must intentionally set up personal stones of remembrance. This helps shift my selective memory to simply remember who God is and how He's operated in my life. Can you relate?

For instance, there is some pain associated with the memory of my father's addiction and all that my family experienced because of it. Yet my stone of remembrance for that time is how the Lord saved my dad and gave me the sweet memory of us in church worshiping together.

The last time I saw my dad was in church with my family—what a sweet stone of remembrance that represents Christ's redemptive power in the life of my father. This does not mean I suppress the memory of his addiction because it makes me sad. It simply means I am choosing what I will memorialize in my mind. I am memorializing Christ; I am memorializing His redemptive power.

Others throughout Scripture memorialized God's redemption. One was the prophet Samuel, who was known for anointing both Saul and David as king over Israel. Soon after he was called by the Lord as a prophet, he had to lead and encourage the Israelites, who were experiencing terror from the Philistine people. Samuel called God's people to get rid of their foreign gods and idols, to dedicate themselves to the Lord and to worship only Him (1 Sam. 7:3). He offered sacrifices on their behalf and prayed for God to deliver them from the Philistines as they approached to attack. Then we see the Lord literally confuse their enemies so that Israel could defeat them.

> *Afterward, Samuel took a stone and set it upright between Mizpah and Shen. He named it Ebenezer, explaining, "the* Lord *has helped us to this point." So the Philistines were*

> subdued and did not invade Israel's territory again. The
> LORD's hand was against the Philistines all of Samuel's life. (1
> SAM. 7:12–13)

This moment in Samuel's life of raising this stone and naming it "Ebenezer," which means "stone of help," can be significant for us today. How many times can you remember the Lord helping you through a tough season? What comes to mind as you think of your own "stones of help" or "Ebenezers"?

As we are preparing to raise our own Ebenezers, let's talk about some general things that are worth remembering. Perhaps this can trigger your memory as we reflect throughout this chapter.

The Lord Answers Prayer

I know this is a book about growing in intimacy with God through unanswered prayer, but I need you to remember this if you don't take anything else from this book. *God does answer prayer!*

Yes, even if you are sitting in the chasm between a prayer and an answer, more than likely you are sitting in an answered prayer! Sometimes we forget that, especially when we have a longing for something else. And although that longing is real and valid, we can still be intentional with remembering that we do serve a God who hears us and answers prayer. "Without faith it is impossible to please God, since the one who draws near to him must believe that he exists and that he rewards those who seek him" (Heb. 11:6).

Remembering answered prayers of the past helps build our faith and belief. It also reminds us that He rewards those who diligently seek Him. Oftentimes we don't know how the answer will come or what it will look like. We can still rest, knowing that He will answer. And what God has for us is better for us than even our own desires.

Earlier I shared about my brother Rick, sister-in-law Shawn, and my niece Grace, who was born with a developmental disability. Rick and Shawn were given grim statistics such as the estimated mortality rate for her condition: 34 percent within the first two years of life. In fact, the doctors suggested that they abort her due to the disability that she would be born with.

They were told she would never eat by mouth and would have to receive nourishment through a gastrotomy tube. Last, they were warned that Grace might never walk or communicate, and that she would continue to have consistent seizures.

But God had other plans! We see the goodness and grace of God in my niece every day. She has lived past the age of two and enjoys her food by mouth daily. Through consistent therapy sessions, her legs have strengthened to the point that she is able to stand and take some steps with the help of a walker. And this is just the beginning! She is also learning how to communicate through a special device.

Sometimes we expect the answered prayer to come in an instant miracle. And yes, God can do that because, well, He's God. But oftentimes, the answered prayer is simply His extended grace together with our faith, trust in Christ, and our part of working out. For my niece the working out has come via therapy sessions and her parents choosing to trust the Lord daily with her life. Grace has brought such joy to our lives and has been a gift to our family. Every moment our family spends with her we see that her life has great purpose.

May we be encouraged to know that God is in the details of our life and desires to receive glory from each part. Every time we get to enjoy my niece, we fully know that it is the Lord who has given her to us and continues to grace her parents daily as they care for her well.

What are the unexpected or even expected faith-filled answers to prayer you've experienced?

As I'm writing this section, I am with my mom in the hospital. She came here with a temperature of 105 and, with her being immunocompromised, any sign of infection can be scary. In situations like these it's easy for our minds to drift into the worst-case scenario. This is especially true when your mind can remember a worst-case scenario.

Last year we were here, and these symptoms exposed that my mom was fighting sepsis. Even with that memory, I had to remember how the Lord brought us through, and He can do it again. And you know what? He did! My mom was released from the hospital tonight, and this time was different. I raise an Ebenezer!

The Holy Spirit Is Here to Comfort

"The Counselor, the Holy Spirit, whom the Father will send in my name, will teach you all things, and remind you of everything I have told you" (John 14:26). "Counselor" in this verse is also rendered as Advocate, Helper, and Comforter in different versions of Scripture.

The Holy Spirit is the person who helps us grow to look more like Christ. He convicts, and He is also our comforter. Can you recall a situation where it feels like everything is crashing all around you, but for some odd reason you are experiencing peace? Or you can be experiencing a situation where everyone else is anxious or fearful, yet you are okay? This comfort is brought to you by the Holy Spirit who is there producing warm security in the midst of the most chaotic situations.

When have you recently experienced the comfort of the Holy Spirit? I immediately think back to the moment I got the news about my father's passing. Yes, I was hit with the unimaginable grief that comes with the loss of a loved one. I also experienced peace that surpassed my human understanding; a supernatural peace that comforted my soul. We must remember the ways that the Holy Spirit is here, leading, guiding, and comforting us as we navigate the tension of unanswered prayer.

The Lord Loves You

This may seem like a matter-of-fact or clichéd statement, but let's unpack why we need to raise our Ebenezers here.

As we walk through seasons of life that feel barren, lament dreams that seemingly have fallen apart, or feel absolutely alone in our experiences, all while traversing through wilderness, it's easy to "feel" unloved. I think it's because our natural inclination is to equate love with the warm, butterfly feelings that a new romantic love may bring.

The way God loves His creation has nothing to do with these feelings, though. His love is based on a choice. He has chosen to love us in spite of our sin. He loves us so much that He gave His only Son, and that whoever believes in Him will not perish but have everlasting life, as John 3:16 assures us.

And although this verse is ingrained in many of us from Sunday school memorization exercises in childhood, it's easy to forget when we feel unloved and unseen. It can be easy to forget that we are loved when the prayers of others are being answered around us and we still wait. As a practice, then, we must intentionally remember the truth of the gospel, raising Ebenezers quite often as we reflect on how the love of Christ has saved us.

As I walked through the hardship of infertility, remembering that I am loved and reflecting on how the gospel has changed my life helped my perspective. Simply put, we serve a God who identifies with pain because of the pain He experienced through His death on the cross. He not only sympathizes but has compassion for the suffering we experience in this world as a result of the fall in the garden of Eden. And if we allow Him, He will love us through it by the power of the Holy Spirit. So let's raise our Ebenezers! How has the love of Christ changed your life? It is this same love that has the ability to restore and refresh our souls over and over again.

The Lord Renews

In those moments when our internal battery needs a jump, time in the Lord's presence gives us exactly what we need to go on.

Today, I found myself scrolling my phone as I looked at the news cycle of current events. At the time of this writing, thousands of people have been impacted by massive wildfires spreading through Southern California, leaving devastation in their wake. Countless individuals have lost their homes, even those whose prayers to see them spared were not answered with a yes. Many will have to rebuild.

But before any of us can rebuild a dream that fell apart, we must allow the Lord to renew our strength. When you've experienced suffering, hardship, or trauma, your soul can simply feel beaten down by it all. This is important to remember, because this world and all that it brings can have the power to drain our battery if we allow it.

As I join the rest of the country in lamenting the California wildfires, I pray that those who already know Christ will find a renewal of strength in their moment of solitude.

In 1 Kings 19, the prophet Elijah is on the run to escape the wrath of an evil queen, Jezebel, wife of Ahab (if you're not familiar with why he's fleeing the wicked queen, read about Elijah on Mount Carmel in 1 Kings 18. It's a readable and entertaining story!). Elijah traveled for a day into the wilderness. Then he "sat down under a broom tree and prayed that he might die" (1 Kings 19:4).

In a moment of Elijah's deepest despair, God sends provision through an angel who furnishes food and drink for him. After eating and drinking, he takes a moment to rest and receives strength to continue his journey in the wilderness over the next forty days. Elijah walks to Mount Horeb where He experiences an encounter with the Lord, who speaks to him in a soft whisper.

> *A great and mighty wind was tearing at the mountains and was shattering cliffs before the LORD, but the LORD was not in the wind. After the wind there was an earthquake, but the LORD was not in the earthquake. After the earthquake there was a fire, but the LORD was not in the fire. And after the fire there was a voice, a soft whisper.* (1 KINGS 19:11–12)

You might have heard of the "still, quiet voice" from the Lord; this is the passage that phrase comes from.

The Lord gives Elijah specific instructions at that time. We can find much to learn about the renewing power of the Lord through this story. First, we must not take for granted His ability to renew us by simply taking care of our bodies through rest and nourishing our bodies through good food. However, bread alone is not enough to complete the renewal process. "Just as sure as Elijah needed food and rest, he also needed time in God's presence to get his spiritual feet back under him."[2]

:: **TAKE A MOMENT**

How have you experienced God's renewing power in your life in the moments where dreams have seemingly fallen apart? How have you seen the Lord give you a new dream, fresh hope, and continued strength for the journey?

I raise an Ebenezer as I've watched the Lord renew my mother's strength as cancer returned to attack her body. Even now, He's renewing her strength to live another day as she does her part to fight this disease while trusting the Lord to do the rest.

:: **TAKE A MOMENT**

What will you memorialize in your mind? I challenge you to use this year to write twelve personal memorial stones. At the end of each month, write down something you remember about God and His character. How did you see God operate in and through your life? I know that as you do this, it will be easy to go over twelve. And that's great. The goal is to simply get into the habit of memorializing what we know about God and who He is as we walk through what's hard.

The Power of Storytelling

Many of the stories in Scripture and throughout history have been passed down to generations orally through storytelling. This has been a way cultural traditions and experiences have been remembered for centuries. During the Middle Passage, Africans carried culture and traditions with them through storytelling and songs that had been told for generations. Scholar Darwin Turner writes, "Since the middle and late nineteenth century, recognition has been given to two manifestations of the oral tradition in African American culture—the folk tales and the folk songs, including, of course, the spirituals."[3]

I don't know all the science behind this, but it is proven that telling stories helps us to remember. "Stories evoke emotions. When we're emotionally engaged, our brains release neurotransmitters like dopamine and oxytocin, which enhance our ability to encode and recall memories," research has found.[4]

It is important to assess, "What stories am I telling myself about my life and God's role in it?" The stories we are telling ourselves and our families will shape what we remember for generations to come. Some of my most treasured times were sitting on my grandmother's bed as I listened to her tell me stories of her upbringing. And although there were some hard things she went through, what I remember most are the things she shared about how the Lord kept them. I remember her resilience and how the Lord answered prayers in her life. I remember the stories of how my family's dreams seemed to be falling apart but the Lord birthed new dreams that served our family.

Over the years, it was these stories that would shape how I began to trust the Lord in my own life. Today, I can recount story after story of how the Lord not only kept my family but performed various miracles and showed up in ways we did not expect. Recounting these stories and sharing them creates our own oral traditions in how we will see God and ourselves during difficult times.

In church while I was growing up, we had "testimony services." Members of the congregation getting up to testify by sharing how the good Lord had brought them through a test or a trial. These services showcased the power of storytelling because every time you would leave one, you were not only inspired but empowered to live by faith as you serve the Lord.

I think it would be beautiful to see these types of services return in our local churches as we collectively fight to remember the goodness of God in a world that fights hard to make us forget.

⁝⁝ TAKE A MOMENT

> Pray these words out loud: "Lord, help me remember Your great mercy and love. Help me remember how You've shown up in my life and in the lives of those around me. Help me remember Your comfort and how You have strengthened me through the most challenging of times. Help me remember who You are as I wait and trust You to answer my prayers according to Your perfect will. Help me remember that Your perfect will has always turned out for my good and Your glory. In Jesus' name, Amen."

9

Rebuild

> *They said, "Let's start rebuilding," and their hands were strengthened to do this good work.*
>
> NEHEMIAH 2:18

YOU'VE MADE IT THIS FAR! The sun is beginning to peek through the clouds.

Let's take stock of where we are. You've probably traversed some wilderness and valley seasons. You may be healing from a miscarriage or other major loss. You were laid off from your dream job, but perhaps you are ready to entertain other opportunities. You went from watching a church online to slowly visiting churches after recovering from spiritual abuse. Maybe you are healing from the betrayal in a friendship or in a relationship.

Or perhaps, you received a good report from the doctor after battling chronic disease.

Things are beginning to turn around.

Or maybe you aren't quite there, and you are just in the space where you are renewed because you have received strength from the Lord. You've been leaning into His grace and casting your cares on Him: "Those who trust in the LORD will renew their strength; they will soar on wings like eagles; they will run and not become weary, they will walk and not faint" (Isa. 40:31).

Some say the Lord won't give us more than we can bear, but this is a mistaken teaching. God actually does allow more on us than we can bear because it is not our responsibility to carry the burden. When life feels heavy and the weight of whatever it is we are trusting the Lord for feels overwhelming, it is up to us to cast all our cares upon the Lord, knowing that He cares for us (see 1 Peter 5:7).

These are the opportunities for us to put away our superhero capes and let go of the idea that we have to be the strong one. Jesus reminded Paul, who described having a "thorn in the flesh," that "my grace is sufficient for you, for my power is perfect in weakness" (2 Cor. 12:7, 9).

Wherever you are, if you have received a yes to an answered prayer, a not yet, a no, or simply just find yourself continuing to wait on the Lord, there is a chance you may need to rebuild some areas of your faith. And for that to happen, you may need to check your faith toolkit.

If you are like me, these seasons of life can take a lot out of you to the point of even cracking the very foundation on which you stand.

The Foundation

We must remember that we are people with a soul, and if we are in Christ, we are a temple for the Holy Spirit. This means from the day of our conversion, we are building a spiritual foundation that anchors our souls. Jesus talks about the importance of a strong foundation in Matthew 7:24–27:

> "Therefore, everyone who hears these words of mine and acts on them will be like a wise man who built his house on the rock. The rain fell, the rivers rose, and the winds blew and pounded that house. Yet it didn't collapse, because its foundation was on the rock. But everyone who hears these words of mine and doesn't act on them will be like a foolish man who built his house on the sand. The rain fell, the rivers rose, the winds blew and pounded that house, and it collapsed. It collapsed with a great crash."

The building blocks of our foundation in Christ involve hearing the word of God *and walking out those words* in obedience to the Father. The more we live out our faith through obedience, the stronger our foundation in Christ becomes. These foundations can weaken or crack at times. Usually these cracks are subtle, and they creep in from areas of sin or simply our own disappointments with Christ may taint our view of His character.

How would we know if we have a cracked foundation? Here are a few questions to ask ourselves as we assess where we are spiritually:

- How were you affected in the midst of your desire or dream falling apart?
- Were there times where you found yourself being double-minded? These are the moments where you prayed and yet shortly afterward you were doubting.
- Did you ever question if God was truly good?
- How did or how are you coping as you wait for the Lord to answer?

- Do you find yourself coping through unhealthy ways like mindlessly scrolling on social media, binge-watching television, or indulging in harmful habits?
- Did you try to take things into your own hands and are now living in the consequences of that decision?

These questions are not an attempt to shame you. These are simply the questions that I've had to answer as I examined myself and came honestly before the Lord about where I was. I realized that my answers to these questions revealed that I had made the dreams for my life an idol. When the dreams looked as if they were crushed, it shook my foundation to the core.

Later on, I realized I was not clinging to Christ the way I needed to. In areas of my life I may had been vigilant to protect before, I had begun to let my guard down. I was not allowing Christ to fill the void of being without a child, and for years, I coped in the power of my own strength.

Perhaps you found yourself not allowing Christ to fill the void of loneliness and you made some decisions that weren't led by Christ but by your own desires. If you are in this place, let's look at some helpful ways to rebuild.

Repairing the Cracks

In thinking about how foundations are rebuilt there is one process that resonated with me as it pertains to rebuilding our spiritual foundation. This process is called underpinning. Underpinning is the process of digging down to install concrete piers beneath an existing foundation to provide additional support and stabilize any settling issues. It is used in construction when a foundation is sinking. When a spiritual foundation is shaken, broken, or sinking, it may be helpful to assess our support systems moving forward.

> **∷ TAKE A MOMENT**
>
> Are we allowing ourselves to be in a healthy, Christ-centered community? Or did we isolate ourselves? Do we have friendships in our lives that are healthy and point us to hope when it feels like there is none? Do we have people in our corner who will lament when it's time to lament and rejoice when it's time to rejoice?
>
> We may also take a look at where we are with our spiritual disciplines. Are we doing the work of the ministry more than allowing ourselves to be ministered too? Are we praying, reading, and studying the Scriptures? Are we taking time to go on a fast as needed?

Things like having good friends and a healthy, Christ-centered community may be "matter of fact" to the Christian who is having the type of season where all of their needs are met and their desires are fulfilled. However, when you are in a place of uncertainty, these areas may become foggy through our personal disappointments.

During my battles with infertility—and even now through my mom's battle with cancer—I must constantly remind myself of the character and nature of God. This is one of the reasons I wrote this book: to serve as a tool to remind those who are in the valley and walking through the wilderness of who God is as He walks with them. It can be used to stabilize those of us who are feeling shaky because we don't understand why things are happening the way they are. I present this book to offer hope and serve as a reminder that our God, who is sovereign, knows us best and, like a good Father, is always working out things for our good.

It is to remind us to trust the perspective of the One who sits high, knows our futures, and knows how we are to be used for His glory during our lifetime.

> *If we are going to rebuild a crack in our foundation, we are going to have to get vulnerable with the Lord and with each other on where we truly are.*

So yes, we all may need some underpinning from time to time, which will require us to dig beneath the surface and be honest with ourselves about where we are with the Lord. Am I secretly angry with God and trying to cover up my true emotions with church work or "Christianese" in my conversations? For example, when someone asks, "How are you doing?" you are answering with phrases like "blessed and highly favored" when you don't feel blessed at all. If we are going to rebuild a crack in our foundation and dig our roots deeper than before to stabilize ourselves, we are going to have to get vulnerable with the Lord and with each other on where we truly are.

As I think of my own journey of rebuilding the cracks in my foundation, I think of the Jewish remnant who had survived the exile in the book of Nehemiah.

Nehemiah was an Israelite leader who served as King Artaxexes' cupbearer in the Persian court. So his job was to serve wine at the king's table and taste anything before it was served to the king to protect him from being poisoned.

Nehemiah learned from his brother Hanani that those who had survived the exile were in great trouble and disgrace, and that Jerusalem's wall had been broken down and its gates had been burned (Neh. 1:3). With Jerusalem's wall being destroyed, this left an already vulnerable group of people even more vulnerable. Nancy Wolgemuth explains, "This news was cause for grave concern, for the walls and gates of ancient cities provided necessary protection from enemies. A community whose walls and gates were broken down was vulnerable and defenseless against attack."[1]

As we seek to rebuild spiritual walls of protection in our lives, we can learn principles from Nehemiah about God's role in the lives of those who must rebuild.

Feel the Feelings, Pray the Prayers

When Nehemiah heard about what was happening with those who survived the exile, he did not immediately rise to action. We see his humanity on display as he took the time to feel all the things. Nehemiah 1:4 says, "When I heard these words, I sat down and wept. I mourned for a number of days, fasting and praying before the God of the heavens." As we learned earlier, lament is both biblical and emotionally healthy. The Lord isn't looking for robots to walk out our obedience to Him without any feelings. Sitting in the places of the unknown as we wait for the Lord to answer specific prayers can feel hard. It's also hard when we realize that there are areas of our spiritual foundation that may need some strengthening.

Fasting from things you're leaning on for a small measure of comfort can allow you to turn to the Comforter and lean in on the comfort of Christ.

So yes, feel the feelings—but then pray the prayers. Nehemiah knew that He served the God who keeps His word, and I believe you know the same. We all have a history with the Lord that should remind us God does answer prayer even if it's not within the timing we desire.

But Nehemiah did not just lament and pray. He also fasted before the Lord. This means he refrained from all food and drink to truly focus on prayer and hearing from the Lord.

Today, we are overwhelmed by many distractions that are constantly seeking to chip away at our focus on the Lord and His voice. As we seek to rebuild a cracked foundation with the Lord, fasting is a spiritual discipline that would be healthy to incorporate. There are many ways to fast, and I encourage you to think about what you may be giving an unhealthy amount of attention to. You may have found yourself numbing pain through social media or emotional eating. You may turn to entertainment, zoning out while swishing through options on Netflix. You may avoid being alone with your own thoughts—avoiding silence and solitude. Fasting from things you're leaning on for a small measure of comfort can allow you to turn to the Comforter and lean in on the comfort of Christ. Perhaps this may lead you to something specific you can fast from as you pray.

> **⁞⁞ TAKE A MOMENT**
>
> When was the last time you fasted and prayed? What have you given an unhealthy amount of attention to, e.g., social media, television, certain foods? Pray and seek the Lord if there is anything that you need to fast from and then plan to walk this out.

Determine What's Really Broken

The way cracks are formed in a foundation differs depending on the situation or the environment during which the crack was created. With houses, foundations may crack because of poor workmanship, drainage issues, earthquakes, sinkholes, or any number of reasons or events. In a similar way, not all cracks in the foundations of our faith have the same root causes or make an appearance the same way.

Losses, Disappointments, Unanswered Prayer

Just a cursory glance at headlines in the news or acquaintance with people going through extraordinary hardships can lead us to wonder, Why would God allow this to happen? Does God even care? And to be sure, people of faith ask these questions.

In the book of Job we encounter a man who walked uprightly and feared the Lord. He experienced immeasurable losses that included property and children (Job 1:13–22). Job also experienced health challenges that were so horrible his wife eventually wondered why he didn't just give up. She asked, "Are you still holding on to your integrity? Curse God and die!" (Job 2:9). I understand how she could feel this way. This is a woman who is grieving the loss of her children. She has also suddenly lost everything, including their way of life. Life can feel cruel.

What was behind these tragic events? In Job chapter 1, we learn that Satan, our adversary, suggested to God that Job was only righteous because of his immense blessings. Satan suggested that if Job lost everything, "he will surely curse you [God] to your face" (v. 11).

God gave permission for Satan to torment Job, but only as far as God allowed.

> "Very well," the LORD told Satan, "everything he owns is in your power. However, do not lay a hand on Job himself." So Satan left the LORD's presence. (JOB 1:12)

Tony Evans makes this comment about this situation: "God drew the line where Satan had to stop; he maintained authority over the evil one. In his grace, God limits our trials. God's goal was to purify and sanctify Job, not to take him out."[2]

The story of Job and what happens here is something that has always been challenging for me to process because Job is an example of when bad things happen to people through no fault of their own. Job was described as "a man of complete integrity, who feared God and turned away from evil" (1:10). Think about someone you truly love and the heavy losses they may have encountered. No one likes to see that happen. Or maybe your own story comes to mind if you are experiencing a disappointment or loss that you truly did not expect.

Let's review some things about God through the story of Job that may help us when the cracks from loss and disappointment are a part of our lives. "The book of Job demonstrates that a sovereign, righteous God is sufficient and trustworthy for every situation in life, even in the most difficult of circumstances." It teaches that "suffering comes to everyone, the righteous and unrighteous alike.... Ultimately, God controls all of life's situations, including limiting the power of Satan.... God's comfort and strength are always available to the trusting soul."[3]

This is not to put a bandage on the wound of a loss. Losses are indeed disappointing. I don't pretend to understand why God allows certain disappointments or even tragic situations to come into our lives. No one has ever been able to perfectly answer that question, though philosophers and theologians have tried.

But what Job teaches us is God has a good plan in the midst of loss. I believe if we sit with this and truly seek the Lord as we walk through what's hard, we can begin to grasp what we are to learn. Most importantly, we can begin to see God working amid a loss. What would happen if our questions to the Lord that exclaim "God, why did You allow this to happen to me?" could turn into declarative statements like "Lord, help me see You in this! I don't understand but help me see what You see."

One thing is certain: His plans always involve making us look more like His Son. And there is no one who understands loss quite like our Father who gave His only Son to take on the sins of the world.

Rebuild with a Team

Nehemiah secured permission from the king of Persia to travel to Jerusalem to begin the project of rebuilding the city's walls. He told the people remaining in the city how the Lord had led him to begin the work; he assembled a team of "those who would be doing the work" (Neh. 2:16). The team responded: "'Let's start rebuilding,' and their hands were strengthened to do this good work" (v. 18).

Very few things can be built with stability and deep roots alone. This is why most building takes place with teams. Individuals gifted in different ways that we are not can help as we seek to strengthen our foundation in Christ.

A Pastor and a Bible Teaching Church

Though we have opportunities to access teaching and discipleship from social media pastors and influencers—and even attend church online—the reality is that we all need someone to pastor us. We need shepherds who offer spiritual covering, who can truly walk with us and our families as we grow in the Lord.[4] I've noticed a significant difference in my own spiritual foundation when we have allowed our family to be shepherded by a healthy leader than when we were without covering.

> *I exhort the elders among you as a fellow elder and witness to the sufferings of Christ, as well as one who shares in the glory about to be revealed. Shepherd God's flock among you, not overseeing out of compulsion but willingly, as God would have you; not out of greed for money but eagerly; not lording it over those entrusted to you, but being examples to the flock.*
> (1 PETER 5:1–4)

A Therapist or Counselor

Some things are better processed with a licensed therapist or counselor. Generationally, seeing a therapist has not been a popular thing to do within communities of color. I am grateful to see those ideas shift over the years as we have learned the benefits of therapy and how its various practices can aid in our overall healing and mindset.

Today, many health insurance plans cover therapy costs. And there are several different types of therapy—EMDR therapy (Eye Movement Desensitization and Reprocessing), trauma therapy, talk therapy—to fit your individual needs. Christian therapists are also available who can help you process things through a biblical worldview while still using the principles of psychology to guide you as you rebuild. Websites like therapyforblackgirls.com and psychologytoday.com can help you find a licensed therapist in your area.

A Truth-Telling Disciple

When we are rebuilding a cracked foundation, we don't need people who simply tell us the things they think we want to hear. "Yes people" are individuals who may overlook areas in your life that need to be brought to the surface. They may wrestle with people-pleasing and simply don't want to say the thing that could upset you. Instead, it is necessary to have a person in our lives who is actively following Jesus and loves us enough to tell us the truth about where we are and things they see in our lives.

This is not to be done to tear us down. In fact, a truth-telling disciple actually builds us up while holding us accountable. They can see the cracks in our foundation, and they help us repair those cracks through building us up with the truth of God's Word. The truth-telling disciple reminds us that we are image bearers, helping us build character in areas in which we may be weak.

During challenging seasons of our own marriage, truth-telling disciples were in our lives reminding us of who we are and what we are called to do together. They saw areas that needed to be fixed that we were rather blind to. At the time, some things were difficult to hear, but looking back, I am grateful for those people who saw cracks that needed to be mended. In the end, we were able to build a stronger foundation.

Begin the Work of Repairing

Imagine a woman who has all the credentials of being a faithful follower of Christ. However, as she takes intentional steps to walk out her calling, it seems like every door is closing in her face. She has prayed and fasted and the wait seems daunting as she finds herself stalled in roles that she is overqualified for. She may ask the question as many of us have asked while waiting for God to answer: "Does He even hear me?" We may even have an answer from God that requires our faith to pivot or to trust Him more deeply, but it's not what we wanted to do. Some may wonder, "Does God even care?" I've been here where I've asked, "Lord, does everything in my life have to be a testimony?"

And these types of questions continue as we experience areas of our faith that are especially trying. I remember watching my husband walk through challenges under church leadership that was unhealthy. At times what we were experiencing was so heartbreaking and stifling that we wondered, *Where is God in all of this?*

However the crack appears in our foundation, it's important that it does not remain there. Have you ever seen a crack on a windshield grow? What may have started off as a small crack from a pebble that fell off a truck in front of you and hit the window will continue to expand if it is not repaired. The more the crack expands, the more costly the repair.

This is why when we notice these cracks within our foundation that cause us to question the very character and nature of God, it's important we take the time to recognize where we are and begin the work of repair.

Reconstruct and Rebuild

It is possible that we may have come into our relationship with God and Christianity with a set of expectations. These expectations were formed during our childhood, through things we were taught over the years, and perhaps even from movies we watched or speakers we heard. Expectations naturally form through our experiences or what we are taught, and they impact all of our relationships whether positively or negatively. Within a marriage we may expect our spouse to make us feel a particular way or do a particular thing. When that expectation isn't met, we may find ourselves questioning the validity of the relationship.

The same thing may happen at times with our relationship with God. Our views of who God is may need to be reconstructed due to unbiblical expectations. These types of expectations have us question the validity of our relationship with Him and His character. As we discussed earlier, God is not a vending machine, and our relationship is not transactional. Grace is a gift from God, and we do nothing to deserve the measure of grace that we receive.

Understanding who God truly is in the midst of unanswered prayer, loss, and disappointments is the best way to begin rebuilding. Who do you say that Jesus Christ is? This is the question Jesus asked His disciples, and it's a question each of us must answer.

> *"But you," he asked them, "who do you say that I am?" Simon Peter answered, "You are the Messiah, the Son of the living God." Jesus responded, "Blessed are you, Simon son of Jonah, because flesh and blood did not reveal this to you, but my Father in heaven."* (MATT. 16:15–17)

⁚⁚ TAKE A MOMENT

If we allow Him, the Holy Spirit will reveal to us the true nature and character of God through prayer. He also reveals His character over and over again throughout Scripture. Take this moment to pray about any cracks within your faith. Confess any anger or disappointment you have in the Lord. He already knows what you are holding. Release it today and pray for His strength and guidance as you reconstruct your view.

When we talk about repairing cracks in our foundation, we must begin with the very foundation of Christ.

For no one can lay any foundation other than what has been laid down. That foundation is Jesus Christ (1 Cor. 3:11).

10

Glory

*Our Lord and God,
you are worthy to receive
glory and honor and power,
because you have created all things,
and by your will
they exist and were created.*

REVELATION 4:11–5:1

I LOVE LISTENING AT THE feet of my elders as they share stories from their past; some are more colorful than others.

I especially enjoyed listening to the stories of my late grandmother, and I still enjoy listening to the stories of my mom and aunts. I love sitting with them as they speak about the 1970s, an era full of Black pride as they donned afros and bell bottoms. They share the soundtrack to their lives that includes Stevie Wonder, The Delfonics, The Stylistics, Aretha Franklin, Earth, Wind & Fire— and many more. As they speak their words, creating movies in my mind, I can't help but smile as they recount their "glory days."

"Glory days" is a term that typically refers to a specific time when someone is very successful. It is also a period in the past that is remembered as a time of great achievement or happiness. In my own life, I too enjoy reminiscing on some of my glory days of the late '90s and early 2000s. The thing about glory days is that it is a term used to think about the great days and times that have passed.

But for the believer, while our everlasting glory days are yet to come, there is still glory to be lived in today.

Glory in the Presence

The glory of God that we read about in the Old Testament is His manifested presence, known in the Hebrew as *shekinah*. Our worship songs today tell of this glory as we sing lyrics like "Let the glory of the Lord rise among us," or "Let Your glory fill this place." Although we cry out to experience God's glory, if God's glory were to truly descend upon us in its full manifestation, we would not survive.

Think about that.

The presence of God is so magnificent that our human bodies and minds cannot fully behold Him, or we would die.

> *Then Moses said, "Please, let me see your glory." He said, "I will cause all my goodness to pass in front of you, and I will proclaim the name 'the LORD' before you. I will be gracious to whom I will be gracious, and I will have compassion on whom I will have compassion." But he added, "You cannot see my face, for humans cannot see me and live." The LORD said, "Here is a place near me. You are to stand on the rock, and when my glory passes by, I will put you in the crevice of the rock and cover you with my hand until I have passed by. Then I will take my hand away, and you will see my back, but my face will not be seen."* (EX. 33:18–34:1)

This is how great God's glory is, and His presence and holiness should not be minimized. God's manifested glory literally stops us in our tracks, and the only thing that makes sense is to simply bow before and worship Him.

> *The temple, the LORD's temple, was filled with a cloud. And because of the cloud, the priests were not able to continue ministering, for the glory of the LORD filled God's temple.*
> (2 CHRON. 5:13–14)

It is a gift to experience a taste of God's glory. To experience Yahweh's glory is to experience His goodness. There will be a time when those who are in Christ will experience this goodness to the full. In biblical times, only the priests of God could enter the temple and experience the presence of God. Even then they were separated by veils or curtains. These veils separated the priest from the holy place and a place called the holy of holies (or, the most holy place) where the ark of the testimony dwelled in the tabernacle. This was as close to God's presence as they could get without dying.

"Hang the curtain under the clasps and bring the ark of the testimony there behind the curtain, so the curtain will make a separation for you between the holy place and the most holy place," God instructed through Moses (Ex. 26:33).

Throughout the book of Exodus, Moses leads the charge, as directed by Yahweh, to build the tabernacle where His glory would reside. The instructions were meticulous and not just anyone could access it. When the construction of the tabernacle was completed the Lord's glory fell upon it: "The cloud covered the tent of meeting, and the glory of the LORD filled the tabernacle. Moses was unable to enter the tent of meeting because the cloud rested on it, and the glory of the LORD filled the tabernacle" (Ex. 40:34–35).

If you read through the book of Exodus, you see how Yahweh's manifested presence appears through a cloud or by fire. Those who walked with or encountered Him were able to experience the shekinah glory or manifested presence of God. Oh, how I have envied witnessing this level of magnificence today!

Indeed, there is beauty in knowing the Lord because there is glory that we have access to and can experience. Although we cannot physically look upon His face or see Him lead us through a cloud or by fire, we can experience His presence through the person and work of Jesus Christ. "The Word became flesh and dwelt among us. We observed his glory, the glory as the one and only Son from the Father, full of grace and truth" (John 1:14).

I love imagining what it would have been like to experience Jesus through His ministry here on earth.

Jesus dwelt among mankind, and those who walked and talked with Him beheld His glory, the glory as the only Son of the Father. On that account Jesus, knowing His expected end, left those who followed Him—and those who would follow after—a gift, the Holy Spirit.

It is because of the death and resurrection of Jesus Christ that we are able to experience the glory of God through the testimony of Scripture and the presence of the Holy Spirit.

I love imagining what it would have been like to experience Jesus through His ministry here on earth. Think about how cool it must have been to sit and hear Jesus preach the Sermon on the Mount. Or to see Him walk through a crowd with His disciples as droves of people tried to get near Him. As I think of those people, I realize that in their lifetime they may have only gotten to experience and behold the glory of Christ once. Today, we have the testimony of Scripture that gives us the opportunity to consistently behold the glory of Christ. And honestly, I think it's easy to take that for granted.

Glory in Scripture

These are not just mere words on a page of a book like the one you are reading right now. The words of Scripture, unlike my words, are living, breathing, active, sharper than any two-edged sword! (See Heb. 4:12.) There is glory to behold on every page as all Scripture points to the testimony of Christ. From the creation account in Genesis we see that the "Word was with God" (John 1:1). In Leviticus as we read through the details of sacrifices, we are reminded of the ultimate sacrifice Christ made on the cross for our sin. In books like Judges and 1 and 2 Kings we are reminded through the sins of imperfect leaders that there would be one perfect leader to come and change everything.

In the Psalms and Proverbs we glean from the wisdom of God while finding words to sing of His glory. Prophetic books like Isaiah and Ezekiel prophesy of His coming. In Matthew, Mark, Luke, and John we get to walk with Jesus through the different accounts of the writers. The epistles such as 1 and 2 Corinthians are like love letters to the church with rebuke, correction, and encouragement. And the apocalyptic book of Revelation tells of the future glory that is to come!

The testimony of Scripture is indeed glorious and good. And we need to be alert to the spiritual warfare that would try to keep us from experiencing this glory. Think about it. How many times are you distracted when you start a Bible reading plan, or just sit down to read or study Scripture? There is glory in the pages of Scripture that the kingdom of darkness does not want you to experience. But when we are aware of what's happening we can be ready to fight against it.

> **⁞⁞ TAKE A MOMENT**
>
> Let's pray: Lord, what distractions are hindering me from experiencing Your glory through the pages of Scripture? Make things clear so that I may remove them. Give me the desire and the strength to know You more deeply through Your words. Your Word says that faith comes by hearing the Word of God. Lord, grow my faith as I grow in Your Word. Strengthen my complete trust in You as I seek You through the Scriptures. In Jesus' name, Amen.

Glory in the Holy Spirit

> *It was now about noon, and darkness came over the whole land until three, because the sun's light failed. The curtain of the sanctuary was split down the middle. And Jesus called out with a loud voice, "Father, into your hands I entrust my spirit." Saying this, he breathed his last.* (LUKE 23:44–46)

"According to the Talmud, the veils were sixty feet long, thirty feet tall and four inches thick. Jewish tradition claims that the veils were so heavy it took three hundred priests to hang them," writes Wybren Oord.[1] (The Talmud comprises Jewish laws and traditions.) This curtain tearing down the middle was not an easy feat. But the weight of what Christ did for us through His sacrifice was not an easy thing. This extremely heavy curtain could have represented the great weight of our sin that separates us from God. Now that the curtain is torn, we no longer need a priest to atone for our sins with the blood of bulls and goats. We have direct access to the presence and glory of God through the Holy Spirit.

The Holy Spirit is the third member of the triune God and, as such, is fully God and fully personal.[2] And the third member of the Trinity is our gift promised to us by Christ for all who believe: "And I will ask the Father, and he will give you another Counselor to be with you forever. He is the Spirit of truth" (John 14:16–17).

The Greek word for Holy Spirit is *parakletos*, which means advocate, mediator, counselor, intercessor, consoler. This means we have the Holy Spirit to walk with us as we navigate life's trials. We have the Holy Spirit to intercede on our behalf as we surrender these prayers to the Lord. And as Counselor and Comforter, we have the Holy Spirit to go to as we walk through losses and disappointments. He is there, waiting for us to involve Him through prayer. We are living through times where we cannot do life without the Holy Spirit.

This week as I prepare to travel, I have had to fight anxiety. Last week two plane crashes happened one day after the next, and one of them occurred out of the airport I frequent when flying. Even if you are in Christ, your humanity feels the weight of all that is happening. These are the moments I find myself praying, "Holy Spirit, have Your way in my life! Help me see You in all of this. I need Your presence! I need Your guidance! I am disappointed and discouraged. Lord, I need You, we need You."

Inviting the Holy Spirit to operate in His roles of Comforter, Counselor, Intercessor, and more has the power to lift the weight that life can bring. The Holy Spirit is the One, the promised gift from Jesus who helps us through every affliction preparing us for the eternal weight of glory. What a beautiful gift it is to have this type of access to the Father.

Glory in Creation

When everything seemingly has fallen apart in our lives, when the dream appears to have died, when the weight of passing time is evident as gray hairs appear on our heads and another New Year's Eve celebration is at hand, it is this glory that we must intentionally press into. Yes, there is much glory to come; but there is also glory to experience here that will keep us going day to day.

We can experience God's glory in His glorious creation:

> *How countless are your works, LORD!*
> *In wisdom you have made them all;*
> *the earth is full of your creatures.* (PS. 104:24)

During one of the most challenging seasons of my life, after receiving news about my mother's health, my husband and I took a road trip to celebrate my birthday. We traveled to a mountainous region in Tennessee and stayed in a luxury treehouse that was so high in the mountains we could see the clouds. In moments of sadness and through tears, we took time to take in the magnificence all around us. God's glory is His goodness.

As we breathed in the mountain air, we simply took in that goodness as we exhaled. Taking in and experiencing God's glory in creation reminds us of how meticulous our God is and intentional in everything He creates. It reminds us that in the larger scheme of things, we serve a big God who has all of this in His hands.

You may not be able to travel to the mountains or take a trip to the ocean. But a simple walk around the block or a bike ride to admire beautiful landscapes in your neighborhood or a trip to a local park may be just what your soul needs. When the weather is nice and I have something heavy on my heart that I am praying about, I love to take a bike ride to Indian Head Rail Trail, not far from where I live. As I bike a few miles, I stop to take in the beautiful scenery, and I pray. I breathe, I pause, I listen. The trail is my special place to truly feel refreshed as I take in God's glorious creation.

> *We enjoy physical benefits by simply going outside and enjoying God's creation.*

We also enjoy physical benefits by simply going outside and enjoying God's creation. God created our bodies to need vitamin D, which we may absorb from the sun, and that positively impacts our immune systems, bone health, and overall mood. Being in God's creation also limits our screentime, always a positive benefit!

> **:: TAKE A MOMENT**
>
> Purposeful moments of taking in God's glorious creation may just be what you need today. Where are your places to take in God's glory in creation? Take a moment now, or sometime this week, to do that. Maybe even take this book and just read and journal somewhere different than you usually do.

Glory in Our Bodies

I experienced body shaming as early as twelve years old. I remember being a little girl experiencing shame as boys in my neighborhood attempted to objectify my body by talking about it or attempting to touch me without permission. As I became an adult, I took ownership of my body in ways that were self-centered, believing it was empowerment. I became hypersexual and used my body as a tool to get what I wanted. Like many, I didn't grow up knowing that God could or should be glorified in my body. I know that some women experience shame with their bodies in other ways, as though feminine features are somehow dishonorable, or that normal sexual desire is a bad thing.

> *As believers, our bodies are temples that house the Holy Spirit.*

But shame was never God's intended plan for our bodies—it was always honor.

In 1 Corinthians 6:15, Paul asks members of the church of Corinth, "Don't you know that your bodies are a part of Christ's body?" He goes on to ask in verses 19 and 20, "Don't you know that your body is a temple of the Holy Spirit who is in you, whom you have from God? You are not your own, for you were bought at a price. So glorify God with your body."

Paul speaks about fleeing from sexual immorality and not abusing our Christian freedom. But as I pondered all of this, I began to dive a little deeper and think of all the reasons why this matters when glorifying Christ.

When I reflect on my past and think of days I gave myself to sexual immorality, I can also think of the moments I didn't take care of my body from what I ate or drank. These actions hindered me from glorifying God due to being distracted, sluggish, and unfocused. I was not honoring the body God had given me or the God who had sacrificed His body on my behalf. I treated my body as if I alone owned it and dishonored myself in ways that didn't honor the glory I carried.

As believers, our bodies are temples that house the Holy Spirit. Our purpose in glorifying God with our bodies protects us from the traps of sin but it is always bigger than us. Jesus desires for His children to be "set apart, useful to the Master, prepared for every good work" (2 Tim. 2:21). We take care of our bodies not for vanity's sake or so we can boast. We take care of and honor them knowing that as temples of the Holy Spirit we have kingdom assignments to fulfill. God's glory is seen through how we honor our bodies as the temples that He lives in within us.

> :: **TAKE A MOMENT**
> What differences have you noticed in yourself as you honored God in your body?

Glory in Sharing the Gospel

> *For God who said, "Let light shine out of darkness," has shone in our hearts to give the light of the knowledge of God's glory in the face of Jesus Christ.* (2 COR. 4:6)

Every day we have the opportunity to invite people in to experience the goodness of God, His eternal goodness through the glorious gospel. We encounter people daily, both those we have relationships with and those we may merely speak to in passing.

As we are dealing with all that comes in our own lives, truthfully, I am not always thinking of the gospel and how to share it. I'm just trying to get to my destination, pick up a coffee order, complete a project with a coworker, or take our daughter to her play gym. I am almost embarrassed by how often I am not thinking of the gift of the gospel but am just going through the routine of daily life. And although I believe we absolutely should share the gospel with people directly, there are ways that our lives open the door for these conversations.

I have learned that how I've shown up, walked through, and endured suffering while clinging to Christ has been a witness to those around me or who've come to know my story. How we continue to live in light of the truth of the gospel as we navigate waters of uncertainty, walk by faith, trust the Lord will answer our prayers is a testimony that gives God glory. The person who is watching you whom you don't even know may come to ask, "How can I get this level of peace?" These questions are an open door for you to share the glorious gospel that keeps you.

> *People are open to listening to people they believe may care about them. As we share truth with compassion, it's important to listen and to be guided by the Holy Spirit as we engage.*

Before I knew Christ, I remember being jealous of my mom. I know, it sounds crazy, but I was. My mom had so much joy and I could not understand it. She was a woman living in one of the toughest parts of DC and married to my dad who, at the time, was deep into drug addiction. Even so, she would be going around the house, praying and praising the Lord with gladness. For the life of me, I could not understand it, but deep down I envied it. I envied it because I desired it. I desired the ability to have that type of joy. I began to have conversations with my mom, and she shared how she could experience this type of joy in the midst of such hardship. It was her assurance and relationship with Christ that kept her. Because of her life, I wanted to know and seek the truth of this gospel. Her light changed my life, and my heart became ready to hear and receive the gospel.

We also have opportunities to engage people with the gospel directly through our conversations. Conversations are necessary because no one likes to feel like they are being "sold" the gospel like a hawker at the county fair. We don't need to sell something that is a free gift from God. People are open to listening to people they believe may care about them. As we share truth with compassion, it's important to listen and to be guided by the Holy Spirit as we engage. People are to be treated with care as we approach these conversations. "I believe in the last days," Preston Perry writes. "God will use his people to set the most rebellious souls free. If we remain faithful with God's truth, he will use us to soften the most hardened hearts."[3]

There are opportunities all around us to simply let our lives shine amid darkness. Living in light of the truth of the glorious gospel allows the glory of God to be visible and evident to those around us. It opens doors for bold, Spirit-led conversations that can be the beginning of life transformation and someone else experiencing the goodness and glory of God.

The Glory to Come

> *For I consider that the sufferings of this present time are not worth comparing with the glory that is going to be revealed to us.* (ROM. 8:18)

A hymn written by Sanford Fillmore Bennet in 1868 is called "In the Sweet By and By."[4] The hymn speaks of a time that believers will meet on a beautiful shore, with no more sorrow, and a blessing of rest. I believe the lyrics of this hymn pull from the truth of Scripture written in Romans 8:18: "For I consider that the sufferings of this present time are not worth comparing with the glory that is going to be revealed to us."

This verse, along with hymns like "In the Sweet By and By," remind us of the glory to come at Christ's return and the final resurrection. Even now we anticipate a future glory as we walk through the sufferings of this present age. Understanding the biblical concept of glory encourages us to live life considering these truths.

Glory days are not just a thing of the past. Glory days belong to those who have trusted Christ. These are days where the grief of all that we are navigating here on earth will be wiped away and we will be reunited with our Father. It is the ultimate fulfillment and dream realized.

The Bible uses "glory" language to refer to the eschatological state that believers will experience after the final resurrection. God will raise the bodies of believers in glory, and we will reside in the abiding presence of God's glory.[5]

> *I did not see a temple in it, because the Lord God the Almighty and the Lamb are its temple. The city does not need the sun or the moon to shine on it, because the glory of God illuminates it, and its lamp is the Lamb. The nations will walk by its light, and the kings of the earth will bring their glory into it. Its gates will never close by day because it will never be night there. They will bring the glory and honor of the nations into it.* (REV. 21:22–26)

Picture this. There will be a day where those who are in Christ will dwell with Him in the new Jerusalem. This city doesn't have a need for a church or a temple because the literal presence of God will dwell with us. The city will be lit with God's glory, and we will get to experience it. Darkness will be a thing of the past. Our pain, tears, longings, and grief will not even be a faint memory because we will be enraptured with the glory of God.

> :: **TAKE A MOMENT**
> Spend some time dwelling on these truths. Isn't the thought of this just amazing?

This is the promise you can be absolutely sure of if you are a believer. Every ounce of pain that we have experienced due to being in a fallen world will be eradicated. We will enter into God's eternal kingdom, where we will dwell with Him. Every tear shall be wiped from our eyes, and death, grief, and pain shall be no more. Death does not win! There is glory to behold.

> *Look, God's dwelling is with humanity, and he will live with them. They will be his peoples, and God himself will be with them and will be their God. He will wipe away every tear from their eyes. Death will be no more; grief, crying, and pain will be no more, because the previous things have passed away.*
> (REV. 21:3–4)

Although there are moments here on earth where the blessing of heaven kisses those on earth, it will never fully satisfy our inner longing. This is because eternity is written on the hearts of all mankind (Eccl. 3:11).

When my father passed in 2017, I began to research and read about heaven. I had to remind myself that eternity is real and that there is a life beyond any pain we experience here on earth. As I meditated on Christ and on eternity, my longing for the Lord's presence increased even beyond the longing to see my earthly father again. Those who are in Christ are called to set our minds on things above, not on earthly things (see Col. 3:2).

May the sweet anticipation we feel during the evening before a big event in our lives be how we feel daily when we think of being with Jesus.

It's hard to focus on the truth that we know as Christians when we are in the thick of earthly challenges. If we aren't careful, we may even become indifferent to this truth. As a human being it is easy to focus on the things in front of us that are impacting our minds, heart, and emotions. Living in light of eternity doesn't mean that we become oblivious to our real-life problems or the prayers we hope will be answered here. It means that even as we pray, as we wait, as we grieve, as we hope, we know that there is a greater reality we will one day behold.

I lament that my father died without having met his grandchildren.

I lament watching my mother walk through this ugly cancer.

I lament over the children I miscarried and still long for them.

I lament that in my mid-forties there are things that may not happen for me the way I desired.

Yet as I lament, I purpose myself to remember glory.

Our stories do not end here and that's a good thing.

This is redemption.

Yes, the prayers of the righteous are being answered daily. He knows our wanderings, hears our cries, and sees our tears. He is with us in the tension, and His Spirit is present with us in the moments when His voice seems faint. As a master rebuilder, He takes dreams that have fallen apart and births new dreams and vision inside us. With each challenge He is steadily shaping us to reflect more of His image for the good of others and until the glory of Christ. And, in Christ, we are able to experience a level of fulfillment even as we pray, petition, and wait.

With eternity set in our hearts there is a deeper longing we will always have. May the meditations of our hearts lead us to think on and seek this glory, the goodness of God forever.

Epilogue: The Other Side

OVER THE COURSE OF ELEVEN years of marriage we experienced two miscarriages and infertility. On August 15, 2023, our daughter Justice Joy was born. We had walked the journey of praying for a child and seeing our dreams fall apart with every negative pregnancy test year after year. We lamented the possibility of not having children while seeking the Lord for strength to be content with our portion. There were times we celebrated all the amazing things the Lord was doing in the lives of others, while battling our own feelings of frustration of what we had not yet experienced come to pass.

Although the way this prayer was answered was not how we would have planned it, today we are living in the joy of answered prayer. Today we see what it's like to have God give us a new dream, which turns out to be just the dream we needed.

We are still living in the tension of many unanswered prayers in other areas of our lives. So we continue to trust the Lord, walk by faith, and present our requests to Him, believing that His perfect will is to be done.

But I've learned something about the other side of answered prayer.

As I sat up with my daughter in the wee hours of the morning nursing her, with barely any sleep due to her cluster feeding, I looked at my answered prayer and wept. The tears were a mix of joy, frustration, and the exhaustion that I'm sure all new parents relate to. For over forty years I was able to sleep for eight hours or more each night and had never been a morning person. Now I was getting a few hours a day as I nursed my precious answered prayer every two hours. At that moment I recognized that with all answered prayer comes responsibility and stewardship.

Think about it. With every prayer the Lord answers in our lives, there is then a responsibility on our parts to steward the gift He's given us. Stewardship is not always an easy thing to do. There are challenges. This has been a challenge for mankind from the beginning of time. When Adam received the gift of Eve his response was one of awe:

> *This one, at last, is bone of my bone*
> *and flesh of my flesh;*
> *this one will be called "woman,"*
> *for she was taken from man.* (GEN. 2:23)

Adam eats the fruit from the tree of the knowledge of good and evil after God told them they could have everything in the garden but that fruit. Adam failed to steward the gift of the garden of Eden and his wife Eve well. Instead of leading her back to the words of the Lord, he chose to listen to the words of the serpent. After committing this grave sin, he blames his wrongdoing on Eve, the good gift God had given him:

> *"Did you eat from the tree that I commanded you not to eat from?"*
> The man replied, *"The woman you gave to be with me—she gave me some fruit from the tree, and I ate."* (GEN. 3:11–12)

Eve is not innocent here because she listened to the words of the serpent and invited her husband to do the same. It was at that moment they lost the gift of the presence of God. Glory was removed from them at that moment, and it would be centuries until Christ came to bring restoration.

It is the nature of man to receive a gift from God, an answered prayer, and then wrestle with gratitude or the added responsibilities of stewardship that this gift may bring.

With every answered prayer there are more opportunities to trust Yahweh at another level. This is because our goal is to not become enamored with the gift to the point of idolatry.

I absolutely love being a mom. This is a dream I have waited for and it's here. Yet I find myself having to surrender the temptation to make motherhood an idol in my life. The temptation lurks daily to become so wrapped up in this gift that I don't fully devote my life to the Giver. We will quickly learn that our answered prayers don't always bring us joy, they won't always strengthen us, and some days we may question the answer to our prayer. This is why our dependence must remain on our true source, the gift-Giver, Jesus Christ.

I don't know what that answered prayer is for you. Maybe you finally got the dream job, or the ring on your finger, or you are finally completely cancer free. Praise the Lord!

And always remember the desperation you had for Christ at your lowest point—how you cried out for Him before you got out of bed in the morning. Remember how you sought Him in the evening and prayed throughout the day. Friends, remember and keep this same energy when you are at your highest. It will serve and keep you well.

Through the valleys, wilderness, and mountaintops, remain intimate with the One who carries you through it all.

Acknowledgments

WITHOUT ALL OF YOU, THIS book would not have been written. Thank you to my literary agent, Rachel Jacobson at Alive Literary. You saw something in me and helped me develop ideas before I even became your client. I am forever grateful. Thank you to my acquisitions editor Trillia Newbell, my developmental editor Pam Pugh, and the entire team at Moody Publishers. Thank you for believing in this message, for your encouragement, and partnership along the way.

Yana Jenay Conner, thank you for helping me with my initial book proposal and for coaching me through that process. I really appreciate you. To Ruth Buchanan, you have been the best writing coach. Our sessions pushed me past writing blocks, and you helped me make sense of my thoughts as I wrote. You have an incredible gift, and I am grateful you were a part of my team. Thank you!

To my sister friends in the faith, Dr. Sarita Lyons, Pricelis Dominguez, Jackie Hill Perry, Kristie Anyabwile, Rahiel Tesfamarium, Elizabeth Woodson, Ekemini Uwan, thank you. Thank you for answering my questions about writing, random texts for your opinions on things, and for your support in my process.

To Jess Connolly, my friend and the perfect person to have written the foreword. Thank you for your friendship and sisterhood.

My sister friend Ashley Danielle, thank you for answering my random texts about marketing things and for helping me to process ideas along the way.

To my brother Rick and sister-in-law Shawn and friends Sethlina, Erin, and Lauren, thank you for allowing me to share what God has done in your life in this book.

To my mother in love, Delores Sidberry, and my mommy Robin Schumpert. Thank you for being my village. Without you helping me to care for our sweet Justice Joy I would not have had the time to write and meet deadlines.

Thank you, Dr. Bobby Manning and Rev. Lavera Manning, for your support and wisdom as our pastors.

To my love, Jeffrey Tyler. Thank you for your prayers, your listening ear, your encouragement, your support for this book and everything else I do. You are the epitome of a good man!

To every friend, every group chat, my SoulCircles sisters, church family, thank you! Your encouragement in this journey has meant the world.

Last, I am keenly aware of God's mercy and grace on my life. I am thankful to the Lord Jesus Christ for His love.

Notes

Chapter 1: Barren
1. Tony Evans, *The Tony Evans Bible Commentary: Advancing God's Kingdom Agenda* (B&H Publishing Group, 2019), 9.
2. "Bonneville Salt Flats," Utah.com, https://www.utah.com/destinations/natural-areas/bonneville-salt-flats/.
3. *Merriam-Webster*, s.v. "barren," https://www.merriam-webster.com/dictionary/barren.

Chapter 2: Lament
1. Jennifer Lu, "Read the Full Text of Amanda Gorman's Inaugural Poem 'The Hill We Climb,'" CNBC, January 20, 2021, https://www.cnbc.com/2021/01/20/amanda-gormans-inaugural-poem-the-hill-we-climb-full-text.html.
2. Mark Vroegop, *Dark Clouds Deep Mercy: Discovering the Grace of Lament* (Crossway, 2019), 28.
3. F. B. Huey, *Jeremiah, Lamentations*, vol. 16, The New American Commentary (Broadman & Holman Publishers, 1993), 473.
4. John Onwuchekwa, *We Go On: Finding Purpose in All of Life's Sorrows and Joys* (Zondervan, 2022), 27.

5. C. S. Lewis, *A Grief Observed* (HarperOne, 2015), 3.

Chapter 3: Exile

1. You can read more about these events at "When and How Was Israel Conquered by the Assyrians?," GotQuestions.org, https://www.gotquestions.org/Israel-conquered-by-Assyria.html and at "What Was the Babylonian Captivity/Exile?," GotQuestions.org, https://www.gotquestions.org/Babylonian-captivity-exile.html.
2. You can find Maaden Eshete Jones at www.lovemaaden.com.
3. Tony Evans, *The Tony Evans Study Bible* (Holman Bible, 2019), 1211.
4. Evans, 1211.

Chapter 4: Traverse

1. *Merriam-Webster*, s.v. "promised land," https://www.merriam-webster.com/dictionary/promised%20land.
2. Martin Luther King Jr., "I See the Promised Land," http://www.edchange.org/multicultural/speeches/mlk_promised_land.html.
3. African American Heritage, "Marcus Garvey (August 17, 1887–June 10, 1940)," National Archives, https://www.archives.gov/research/african-americans/individuals/marcus-garvey.

Chapter 5: Prodigal

1. *Merriam-Webster*, s.v. "prodigal," https://www.merriam-webster.com/dictionary/prodigal.
2. Leon Morris, *Luke: An Introduction and Commentary*, vol. 3, Tyndale New Testament Commentaries (InterVarsity Press, 1988), 260.
3. This passage is taken from the ESV® Bible (The Holy Bible, English Standard Version®), © 2001 by Crossway, a publishing ministry of Good News Publishers. Used by permission. All rights reserved.

Chapter 6: Manifest

1. "What Does the Bible Say About Divination?," GotQuestions.org, https://www.gotquestions.org/Bible-divination.html.
2. Kate Bowler, *Blessed—A History of the American Prosperity Gospel* (Oxford University Press, 2013), 14.
3. F. L. Cross and Elizabeth A. Livingstone, eds., *The Oxford Dictionary of the Christian Church* (Oxford University Press, 2005), 1579.
4. Bowler, *Blessed*, 20.
5. Bowler, *Blessed*, 141.
6. R. C. Sproul, *Surprised by Suffering: The Role of Pain and Death in the Christian Life* (Tyndale, 2009), 33.
7. Wayne Grudem, *Systematic Theology: An Introduction to Biblical Doctrine* (Zondervan, 2000), 217.

8. Grudem, *Systematic Theology*, 217.
9. Grudem, *Systematic Theology*, 174.

Chapter 7: Promises

1. Kendell H. Easley, "2 Corinthians," in *CSB Study Bible: Notes*, ed. Edwin A. Blum and Trevin Wax (Holman Bible Publishers, 2017), 1840.
2. "The Promises of God," https://www.thesanctuaryofhope.org/single-post/the-promises-of-god.
3. Kristie Anyabwile, *Literarily: How Understanding Bible Genres Transforms Bible Study* (Moody, 2022), 43.
4. Anyabwile, *Literarily*, 45.
5. Anyabwile, *Literarily*, 54.
6. Winfried Corduan, "2 Chronicles," in *CSB Study Bible: Notes*, ed. Edwin A. Blum and Trevin Wax (Holman Bible Publishers, 2017), 654.
7. John D. Barry et al., *Faithlife Study Bible* (Lexham Press, 2016), Psalm 30:5.
8. Richard A. Burridge, "Studying the Gospels," in *Zondervan Handbook to the Bible*, David Alexander and Pat Alexander, eds. (Zondervan, 1999), 545.
9. Donald Guthrie and Stephen Motyer, "The Letters," in *Zondervan Handbook to the Bible*, David Alexander and Pat Alexander, eds. (Zondervan, 1999), 677.
10. Anyabwile, *Literarily*, 138.
11. Guy M. Richard, *Persistent Prayer*, in the Blessings of the Faith series (P&R Publishing, 2021), 46.

Chapter 8: Remember

1. C. H. Spurgeon, "The Pilgrim's Grateful Recollections," in *The Metropolitan Tabernacle Pulpit Sermons*, vol. 16 (Passmore & Alabaster, 1870), 373.
2. Tony Evans, *The Tony Evans Bible Commentary: Advancing God's Kingdom Agenda* (Holman, 2019), 35.
3. Darwin T, Turner, "African-American History and the Oral Tradition," *Books at Iowa* 53, no. 1 (1990): 7–12, https://doi.org/10.17077/0006-7474.1186.
4. "The Power of Storytelling: Boosting Student Memory and Learning," Science L.E.A.F., March 22, 2024, https://scienceleaf.com/the-power-of-storytelling-boosting-student-memory-and-learning/.

Chapter 9: Rebuild

1. Nancy DeMoss Wolgemuth, "The Wall Is Broken Down," Revive Our Hearts, https://www.reviveourhearts.com/articles/the-wall-is-broken-down/.
2. Tony Evans, *The Tony Evans Study Bible* (Holman Bible, 2019), 561.
3. *The Old Testament Handbook* (Holman Reference 2023), 153.
4. This is not to diminish the pain that one may have experienced at the hands of a pastor or church members. In cases of spiritual abuse, there will be

unfortunate seasons when you do not have a pastor. I believe the Lord's grace is available for those who find themselves in that season. Yet instead of remaining comfortable with this reality, I believe it's important to pray and ask the Lord to lead us to the right pastor to shepherd our lives.

Chapter 10: Glory

1. Wybren H. Oord, "The Veil of the Tabernacle," Christian Library, https://www.christianstudylibrary.org/article/veil-tabernacle.
2. Michael A. G. Haykin, "God the Holy Spirit," in *Lexham Survey of Theology*, ed. Mark Ward et al. (Lexham Press, 2018).
3. Preston Perry, *How to Tell the Truth: The Story of How God Saved Me to Win Hearts—Not Just Arguments* (Tyndale Elevate, 2024), 209.
4. "In the Sweet By and By," Sandord Fillmore Bennett, 1868, Hymnary.org, https://hymnary.org/text/theres_a_land_that_is_fairer_than_day_an.
5. Gregory R. Lanier, "Glory," in *Lexham Theological Wordbook*, ed. Douglas Mangum et al., Lexham Bible Reference Series (Lexham Press, 2014).

You finished reading!

Did this book help you in some way? If so, please consider writing an honest review wherever you purchase your books. Your review gets this book into the hands of more readers and helps us continue to create biblically faithful resources.

Moody Publishers books help fund the training of students for ministry around the world.

The **Moody Bible Institute** is one of the most well-known Christian institutions in the world, training thousands of young people to faithfully serve Christ wherever He calls them. And when you buy and read a book from Moody Publishers, you're helping make that vital ministry training possible.

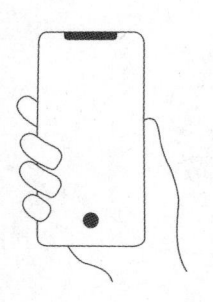

Continue to dive into the Word, *anytime, anywhere.*

Find what you need to take your next step in your walk with Christ: from uplifting music to sound preaching, our programs are designed to help you right when you need it.

Download the **Moody Radio App** and start listening today!

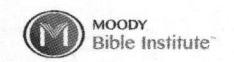

MOODY Publishers

MOODY Bible Institute

MOODY Radio

In a world where people only want to learn how to fulfill their dreams, Jennifer gifts us with a sturdy biblical road map on how to respond and see God at work when dreams fall apart. With truth, compassion, and vulnerability, Jennifer encourages us to be honest about our painful longings while pointing us to Jesus, who faithfully loves, and at times uses the waiting room of life to invite us into deeper intimacy with Him. This book is a healing journey from groaning to glory.

DR. SARITA T. LYONS
Bible teacher, psychotherapist, and author of USA Today's bestselling book Church Girl

For anyone bearing the weight of waiting on God, When Dreams Fall Apart lightens the load.

EKEMINI UWAN
Public theologian and cohost of Truth's Table Podcast

When Dreams Fall Apart invites us to discover what it means to become unabashedly vulnerable in the secret place when our world has been shaken, answers are scarce, and uncertainty abounds. Jennifer Lucy Tyler shows us that persistence in petitioning God when we are overtaken by disillusionment and grief will move God's heart and move us closer to Him than ever before. Jennifer shows us biblically and practically that our grief and questioning have a place of refuge. The more authentic we become in boldly approaching the throne of God in our pain, the less we are concerned about how God answers, and the more we become altogether satisfied with God Himself, who is more than enough. Through the pages of this book, we learn that God hears and sees, that waiting builds our character up to trust in the character of God, and that no matter the season, prayerlessness is not an option.

DR. KANITA RUTLEY
Seed Company, Global Prayer Ministries

Jennifer Lucy Tyler weaves together her deep love for Scripture with her deep experience with grief and triumph to offer us this timely and tender resource. When Dreams Fall Apart is a kind companion for anyone navigating seasons of deferred hope. With biblical truth as the anchor and Jennifer as your gracious guide, you'll find in these pages comfort and courage to press through uncertain paths.

DR. BOBBY MANNING
Author of Gentegration: Connecting Leaders Across Generations